WHAT PEOPLE ARE SAYING ABOUT *SHOWDOWN OF THE GODS*:

"Victor Schlatter has again used his prophetic insight and voice to take on the global community of nations, as far as their priorities are concerned. He did it previously in his book, *Where Is the Body?* as he focused on the Church and Israel. But in *Showdown of the Gods*, Mr. Schlatter calls attention to the evil manipulations of nations in furthering their own interests. His own unique style adds a bit of humor to a very serious discussion of international priorities. In the midst of his analysis of international affairs, Schlatter often illustrates his thesis of national greed and interests by the position that nations take in relationship to modern Israel. His comments on the positions of Islamic nations towards Israel are especially notable, even as he relates these positions to the statements of biblical prophets. Victor Schlatter is to be commended in speaking forth so clearly in *Showdown of the Gods.*"

George Giacumakis, PhD
California State University Fullerton, Professor of History
and Chairman of the Board of the International Christian
Embassy Jerusalem

"Once again the brilliant mind of Victor Schlatter has presented us with a challenging and entertaining book on our current world with Israel never far below the surface. His scientific approach combined with his superb sense of humour and extraordinary knowledge of the content and historical background of the Bible have produced a work even more stunning and provocative than his previous masterpiece, *Where Is the Body?* I thoroughly recommend this landmark work to all Christians and anyone with a real desire to come to terms with the complexities of the ongoing problems in the Middle East."

Geoff Higham
Educational Administrator and School Principal, Australia

"Victor Schlatter's book, *Showdown of the Gods,* like his first, *Where Is the Body?* provokes much thought and hopefully action, as one considers the signs in Israel and beyond that herald a soon coming day of revelation. It is an interesting and even a controversial read, and Victor's easy flowing style makes it an enjoyable one."

Malcolm Hedding
Jerusalem 2001

"In the cold, gray dawn following the 'dot-com bubble,' Victor Schlatter's sobering yet spirited message is a timely warning to all who will listen. The architects of the 'global village' are not following God's plan, and there will be quite literally 'hell-to-pay' as Victor's broad spectrum presentation illustrates. This lively treatise should be read by all who share a concern for where we are headed."

Pete Barden
Retired Vice Chancellor for Admin., University of Colorado at Boulder

"As a Christian media executive, I am concerned that we 'accept' what we do not know and 'know' what we do not understand. I am absorbed by Victor Schlatter's new book, *Showdown of the Gods,* in which he brings out the issues of current media trends and challenges our blind acceptance of stories delivered as fact. From worldwide governmental directions, to environmental, economic and all other global political trends, particularly those issues affecting God's chosen children of Israel at the 'end of times,' Victor prompts us to come back to the truth of God's Word. *Showdown of the Gods* will challenge you to ask yourself some new questions."

Andrew S. Pitchford, Network Station Manager
United Christian Broadcasters, Australia

SHOWDOWN

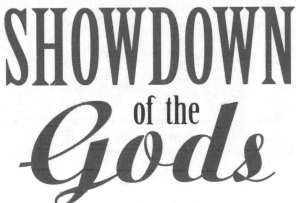

of the

Gods

The Global Confrontation
Between Islam, Humanism,
and God

Victor Schlatter

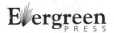

Evergreen
PRESS

ISBN 1-58169-121-1
For Worldwide Distribution
Printed in the U.S.A.

Evergreen Press
P.O. Box 191540 • Mobile, AL 36619
800-367-8203

TABLE OF CONTENTS

To Abba…an offering

INTRODUCTION

Mark Twain once said, "When you find yourself in agreement with the majority, it's time to pause and reflect." And so it is that this book is definitely not going to flow with majority opinion insights. If this were the case, what need would there be for me to write it? The drummer whose beat I find most compelling, usually does not play to please the crowd at large.

And I find this equally true of the God I am prone to serve. He always has appeared a bit out of sync with the masses, and of course, that's why they've tried to revise Him off and on for not a few millennia at least. But by now some of the experts have become so frustrated by the moral intransigence of the Most High, that there is a consensus among those who know what is best for all the rest of us, that He's just going to have to step aside to give a bit of space for a much improved way of doing things.

Well I for one am not quite ready for that, and I'd guess that you may not be either, which meeting of the minds brings us together at this point of time.

Though good old Mark Twain is hardly my role model— he certainly did have a fair bit of clever wit to his credit. Another loner who is a bit more upmarket spiritually was a seasoned prophet named Jeremiah who neither mixed with the majority nor made too many friends because of it. He did have at least two mates (that's a good Australian term for "buddies" and I love it). One was Ebed-Melech, a black Ethiopian who rescued him out of a nasty, mucky pit where the King's honchos left him to die.

Actually he wound up there because he told the truth, which by logic means that the fate of most of our world's crafty politicos will probably never be to get chucked into the mud!

Nevertheless, I am told that the Ancient of Days does have other pits in the planning which feature alternate discomforts slightly worse than a bit of muck!

Anyway Jeremiah had one other helper, Baruch (which means blessed in Hebrew) and he was certainly a blessing to the faithful prophet. He wrote out the messages which God kept giving to Jeremiah, and when the King cynically cut these sacred texts up with his Swiss Army knife, (sorry, it might have been an Israeli blade come to think of it) and pitched them into the fire, good old Baruch wrote them down again. And if he wouldn't have done that, part of our Bible might be still missing today. And he was Jeremiah's good friend as he stood alone—almost alone.

So we have some encouraging precedents for not flocking after the "politically correct" and this book will certainly point us in a much different direction than that which is presumed to be popular.

So come with me on a brief tour around our globe to observe a few of the absurdities they are currently testing in order to upgrade God with a more suitable system. The good news, however, parallels the Almighty's assurance to Job of His power over the raging sea, "This far you may come and no farther; here is where your proud waves halt." (Job 38:11) So as we together wait for the tide to go out for good, let's have a look around us just to be better alerted and prepared to—again like Job—come through as gold!

Victor Schlatter
Migdal, Israel
May 2001

A moment of truth scattered some four score times
throughout the pages of Scripture:

"…and then

will they know that

I AM the LORD."

Cover text: Exodus 3:1-6

CHAPTER 1

Boys Who Play With Buttons

Perhaps we should title this chapter "Big Boys and Their Toys." After getting one's master's degree at Nintendo™ Tech, the bigger and smarter boys in the classroom then move on to such advanced politically-oriented innovations as:

- Panic buttons to prolong one's tenure in political office.
- Eject buttons for the fine art of evading the issues at hand.
- Nuclear buttons (ballistic missiles can be substituted for practice) for when all else fails to keep one's name from being tarnished to the demise of not getting reelected.

It would be a pity at this point not to include a parody created from the style of delightful Dr. Seuss at the height of President Clinton's cross-examination by prosecutor Kenneth Starr. A significantly condensed version of "Dr. Seuss on Lewinskygate," abridged to strictly stick with the potential use of one or more of our above political option buttons goes like this:

Kenneth Starr:
"I am Starr.
Starr I are,

1

    I am a brilliant barri-starr...
    ...And did you tell the girl to lie,
    When called upon to testify?"
President Bill Clinton:
    "That is it, you've gone too far,
    I do not like you Starr you are!
    I will not answer anymore!
    In fact, I think I'll start a war!
    The public's easy to distract,
    When bombs are falling on Iraq!"[1]

But to really zero in on more dignified stuff and get serious about our matter at hand, I would underline that the Bible quite clearly echoes the judgment of immature leadership that is to be cast upon a wayward nation or nations. And might I emphasize at the beginning that this probe of politicians is hardly meant to highlight the unfortunate goings-on of Mr. Clinton above any others on the world setting. But if he happens to meet the criterion for any needed illustration, we will use him.

Over 2700 years ago, a God-oriented ancient named Isaiah ben Amoz from Judea (which land of biblical distinction the Hashemite Kingdom of Jordan contemptuously renamed "The West Bank" in 1967) gave us a few hints of what might happen when His creation gets a bit heady. It's undoubtedly happened a few times since Isaiah spoke up in ages past. Our God is actually big enough to dust off a prophecy and use it as often as He wants. In fact, the more He uses it, the nearer it seems to approach the vortex of His ultimate plans. So perhaps Isaiah's pronouncement was never as applicable and uncomfortably close to final fulfillment as it is in our own day:

I will make boys their officials; mere children will govern them. People will oppress each other—man against man, neighbor against neighbor. The young will rise up against the old, the base against the honorable. A man will seize one of his brothers at his father's home and say, "You have a cloak, you be our leader; take charge of this heap of ruins!" (Isaiah 3:4-6)

Have you ever noticed that the great statesmen of days gone by are becoming somewhat of a collector's item in these times? Many nations today are changing their prime ministers faster than race car drivers change tires. I mean, what has happened to the caliber of leadership which generated the profound quotes of yesteryear? Gone are the Mahatma Gandhis, the Abraham Lincolns, the Teddy Roosevelts and the Winston Churchills who made statements that became profoundly emblazoned as mottoes to inscribe in the wisdom of future generations.

One of the last enduring quotable memorabilia of American presidents was J.F. Kennedy's, "Ask not what your country can do for you, but ask rather what you can do for your country." That's been a while back now. For sure, much of two ensuing generations would have never even heard that quote, let alone identify with the challenge it presents!

These days, we're not hearing too many of the Churchillian-type quotes from the leadership of his native Britain, nor from Europe, Asia, or even from any of the big names in superpower USA. Such is the disappointment in the current scenario of the world leadership of our times.

Of course, we don't want to be too hard on these unfortunate fellows because, admittedly, these are chaotic times, and their jobs are tough. And there are not a lot of extra minutes left over in the day to think up anymore new and witty Ben Franklinisms. On the other hand, that very observation might well reinforce some of our ominous suspicions as to the real reasons for the decline of wise leadership, if not the clues to the unraveling of the world's dwindling hopes. These seem to be the days—in many nations, at least—when voters have a choice between two or more highly polished political figures, each of whose entry into the political arena must of necessity be fortified with copious amounts of cash, and none of whose promises or platforms differ all that much.

How many of these are well-learned but unfortunately otherwise immature aspirants, whose drive in life is mere political passion to occupy the shoes of successful statesmen of bygone years? Moreover, one can only wonder at their true recognition of whether there just might be a Voice out there somewhere with a wee bit more authority above their own. And one soberly reflects, as well, on the wise perception of Lord Acton that power corrupts, and absolute power corrupts absolutely. A bit sad, is it not!

Our sympathies go out to a very clever and promising Mr. Clinton who was a more than sharp university student, who—please forgive my humble but candid analysis—somehow never quite made it over the hump to adult maturity. On the other hand, college kids are cool, so perhaps that's why most of the world—which as you know is becoming proportionally younger both physically and emotionally—responded and still do so graciously to Bill's charisma. Nevertheless, "I didn't do it" somehow doesn't exactly have the ring of making the Top Ten Quotes of the Year for a challenge to future generations. So much for today's great statesmen and their inspirational legacies!

The really good news is that in spite of what today's king

makers lack in integrity, we can breathe much more easily knowing that an escalating number of the world's leaders are now becoming "democratically" elected. A window into that, however, is a recent quote all over the Internet attributed to Stalin that "It doesn't matter who votes, it only matters who counts the votes." Of course, old Joe was hardly a monument of morality, but, at least, he found time to say something—if indeed, he was the one who said it—that was worth remembering. We are living in appalling days.

Let us never sink to the generalization of less than inspiring leadership by focusing on only a few unfortunate efforts in a handful of high profile nations. Scanning east and west, north and south, there's not a great deal to overly excite the imagination in leadership anywhere it seems. When blood curdling terrorists like Yasser Arafat are recycled overnight into illustrious statesmen deemed worthy of the Nobel Peace Prize we're in deep trouble. And, believe it or not, Hizbullah terrorist chief Sheik Nasrallah in Lebanon was also nominated for (but fortunately not awarded) the once illustrious prize by Talab a-Sanaa, one of the 10 Arab members of the Israeli parliament.[2]

In Australia, the country to which I am most closely linked at the moment, we have a late night viewing of the day's Parliament session called Question Time. It is perhaps the most entertaining comedy of the evening. It's an absolute circus to see grown men shouting, screaming and hurling inglorious epithets at one another, all in the name of good government, a privilege earned only by the success of being elected to high office. Our sense of propriety in well-ordered Australian families—propriety becoming an endangered species anywhere in the world—would never permit their children to speak to one another with such rudeness. And, of course, this is a spectacle hardly peculiar to Australia. It is duplicated, I am sure, in free-speech, extolling democracies around the world. Freedom of speech and parliamentary privilege is in quite another league from decency and respect. Boys, of course, will be boys!

These days, in the more "developed" nations at least, the problem of bad manners has been brilliantly solved. This archaic trivia has been long shelved to more relevant concerns of packing automatic weapons in the classroom, hitting the drug circuit and gross perversion of morals—and that before puberty! Could this bear any relationship to the plummeting morals and nonexistent spiritual integrity—and, above all, greed—of the alarming coalition of instability among international leadership? But which comes first, the chicken or the egg? Someone once observed that God gives a nation the sort of leadership that it deserves, and that perception appears not too difficult to accept.

Unfortunately, declining quality of most world leadership is endemic—in Europe, Latin America, in the Philippines, Japan, in Pakistan, throughout Africa, you name it. The once honored statesman descends abruptly from the president's podium directly to the degrading judicial dock in appalling recurrence. If you monitor the news, every one of the nations or continents cited above will turn on a flashing red light. One day the prime minister addresses his nation, the next day he faces a criminal jury. Whether it's because of a merciless media that exults in hounding the heroes, or due to a bullying army that lusts for power, the lads are all at it again, battling for school ground supremacy. Was it ever any different? We can't be sure, but the plague is plainly upon us at this current crisis of history. And we miss Winnie's[3] one liners more than ever.

Finally, the nation that has had its unique foundations in

the arena of not a few other ancient civilizations, again finds itself in the center of world attention. Tiny Israel is the country that has by far the greatest media coverage of annual news in proportionate contrast to its diminutive size and population. The ratio is extraordinarily high. Yet, she, too, has recently had her share of boys playing with their buttons.

At this writing, this minute nation is in the most desperate circumstances of her modern 53-year tenure of rebirth. She has miraculously survived six previous wars—depending on how you differentiate wars and conflicts—foisted upon her by her Islamic neighbors in their impassioned efforts to destroy this unpalatable abomination to Allah. This stems from their bedrock belief of the Koranic-inspired *dhimmi* status of the Jew, and no "peace process" in the world can or ever will change it. Non-world? Perhaps!

Today the threat is far more precarious than in the past. Self-depreciating boys in bright jackets finally politicked their way into authority. They had heard so much, and for so long, from worldwide echoes how deceptive the Jews were to have "stolen" Palestinian land that these new Israeli leaders came to believe this Ursurp's Fable as well. They are inundated with anti-Semitic barrages from the Arabs and the wider petrodollar world beyond, who claim that the ancient Jewish homeland on which Israel now lives was actually stolen "Palestinian" land. The preposterous assertion is, in fact, that it had *always* been "Palestinian" soil for some 5000 years. The claimants unfortunately failed to remember that Abraham (who fathered both the Jews through Isaac and the Arabs through Ishmael) historically happens to be somewhat less than 4000 years old![4]

The new boy leaders (and a few girls) who probably could lay more legitimate claim on Isaiah's prophesy than most other Gentile nations, unfortunately forgot their history as well. Or perhaps they just tucked it under a bushel for the noble sake of a so-called "peace process," which was admirable but not all that brilliant. Had they only even superficially studied the psyche of their Islamic cousins, they would have realized they were dealing with immovable objects and irresistible forces.

And, for sure, they did forget their previous hate-riddled history in which Pharaoh of ancient Egypt enslaved them, and old Nebuchadnezzar of Babylon did likewise. They failed in their deliberations to take into account that another evil Haman planned their genocide, while a diabolical Hitler got even further in attempting to carry it out. They did not remember that the Romans had no problems butchering them, while the more cultured Greeks tried to force them to assimilate and thus blow them away as chaff in the wind. They forgot that world governments will never tolerate for long a nation that has *only one God,* and who refuses to involve Him in back room political deals.

I would appeal for your eyes-wide-open attention at this point. This is what the coming showdown in the Middle East is all about. Israel has never been a nation since the Romans kicked them out of their own legitimate house for the very same reason. If Caesar isn't good enough for power sharing, then the Jews aren't worthy of remaining in town. Ironically, the *jihad* mentality of Islam is far less flexible than even Caesar's, and this is tomorrow in a nutshell, not only for the half of modern Israel who still believe their God, but for all the rest of us who take the Bible seriously.

We must get one thing indelibly clear. We are not talking about individual Jews, individual Arabs or individual anything else. This deals with a confrontation of the *nations* with their own political agendas and *one nation* presumed to be a unique people under the sovereign destiny of the God of the Bible. In fact this is the identity crisis which is currently tearing the nation of Israel apart. Are we going to be Jews of biblical renown, or are we going to be like the rest of the nations?[5] Yet, this is hardly a first time crossroads for what the Scriptures project as "a people who live apart and do not consider themselves one of the nations."[6]

Forgetting history is a calamitous curse. Philosopher George Santayana (1863-1952) postulated: "Progress, far from consisting in change, depends on retentiveness. Those who cannot remember the past are condemned to repeat it."[7] Those well-meaning let's share-the-land-and-have-peace leaders of Israel also forgot their immediate history. They forgot that only 150 years ago the land was a sheer desolation devoid of any major population including so-called "Palestinians."[8] They forgot that for 2000 years no peoples of any culture ever permanently settled the ancient mountains of Judea and Samaria and could regard it as their homeland. They forgot the demographics of history that in spite of the desolation for some 1300 years, there was always a significant Jewish presence scattered throughout their age-old homeland, the land of Abraham, Isaac and Jacob.[9] Instead, they swallowed the "politically correct" propaganda generated merely over the last eight decades by bitter enemies who were determined to "drive them into the sea"!

In childlike naiveté, these well-meaning lads gave their adversaries guns as a "confidence building measure." These boys also thought if only they gave their would-be destroyers some of their own land, the Islamic world would begin to accept them—perhaps even like them. They tried to be nice. Billy Boy Clinton, the free world's greatest statesman (read: salesman), even offered his wisdom and maturity to settle the 4000-year confrontation between Isaac and Ishmael in a projected few weeks—even hours as crunch time approached. Apparently, he never even *knew* the history, much less the Islamic comprehension of peace, which is simply the crushing of an adversary through the violence of *jihad*. The term *Islam* itself means "submission." Guess to whom?

So as it stands today, the "New Middle East" is as old as ever. Not only did their enemies not accept their offer of sharing *part* of their land, they wanted it *all*. PA Chairman Arafat even proposed a new territory they might move to, namely a one-way trip to hell. At least this was the venue suggested for former Prime Minister Barak who ironically offered Arafat above and beyond anything any other Israeli Prime Minister could have ever imagined.[10] Obviously no new love has yet been generated from their age-old antagonists. The more those nice boys offered, the worse it got. In fact, much worse. The *Intifada*—the "uprising" as it is called—began late in September of 2000 and is continuing to escalate. Under the calamitously gullible leadership God allowed them, Israel is now fighting a running battle of violent riots from within, while her not-so-friendly Arab neighbors to the north and east are rattling sabers and racing time in upgrading their long-range missiles with biological, chemical and nuclear warheads from far beyond her tiny borders.

I have detailed this less-than-perceptive juvenile leadership in the Israel scenario with more precision than all the others, but for good reason. The lads at the helm meant well, for sure, but just hadn't done homework as good boys should. Others who knew their Bibles saw the treachery coming. The young men didn't. The Middle East has been the potential flash point for World War III since November 29, 1947, when the United Nations by the narrowest of margins voted to let the Jews return to a minuscule fraction of their ancient homeland. Trying everything else to live in peace with their neighbors, these well-meaning "boys" finally even tried to give a preposterous segment of it away. On February 4, 2001, they were ultimately ejected from their political playground by an unprecedented and humiliating majority of disenchanted voters. But the damage they left behind them is immeasurable.

So "boys will be boys." Have a look across the world scene. These are certainly days of immature leadership in high places—adults in body, razor-sharp in politics, but quite immature in both perceptivity and principle, and most acutely wanting in spiritual values. It is a globe under the guidance of novices who have never learned their lessons—their history lessons, in particular. Quite as we began, Isaiah was more than accurate in his prophecy: "I will make boys their officials; mere children will govern them."

Nevertheless, all this is hardly happening in a vacuum. It is one of a chain of worldwide chastisements for a civilization so advanced in self-esteem that it no longer needs—much less wants—a sovereign God!

1 "Dr. Seuss on Lewinskygate," *The Australia/Israel Review*, AIJAC, Vol. 23, No. 2, 18 February 11 March 1998, Melbourne, Australia.

2 "Nasralla nominated for Nobel Prize," *Jerusalem Post*, October 11, 2000.

3 That is, Winston Churchill.

4 See comprehensive report: *Facts of History*, Stan Telchin Ministries, Inc.6210 N Lockwood Ridge Road #321, Sarasota, FL 34243-2529. See also Joan Peters, *From Time Immemorial*, (New York: Harper & Row Publishers, 1984), pp. 161-163.

5 See 1 Samuel Chapter 8:4-22. Reflect also on the ironic underlying premise of Benjamin Netanyahu, *A Place Among the Nations*, (Bantam Books, New York, NY, 1993).

6 See Numbers 23:9. The entire study of Chapters 23 and 24 of Numbers are an interesting pronouncement from an otherwise pagan prophet.

7 George Santayana, *The Life of Reason or The Phases of Human Progress*, Volume 1 "Introduction and Reason in Common Sense" (New York: Scribner, 1928-1930).

8 Joan Peters, op. cit. pp. 157-161. Also Ramon Bennett, *Philistine* (Jerusalem: Arm of Salvation Publishers, 1995), pp. 147-149.

9 Ibid, pp. 167-171; Ramon Bennett, *Philistine* (Jerusalem: Arm of Salvation Publishers, 1995), pp. 141-143, 146-147, 149-158; Norma Archbold, *The Mountains of Israel* (Joliet, IL: Phoebe's Song Publications, 1993) pp. 25-31.

10 "Congress Urges Bush to Punish PA for Backing Violence: The members of Congress said it was 'inexplicable' that the Palestinians rejected the terms offered at the failed Camp David summit last July, which would have given them virtually all of Judea/Samaria and Gaza and eastern Jerusalem." *Middle East Intelligence Digest*, Jerusalem: April, 2001. See also "The Debate at Camp David Over Jerusalem's Holy Places," *Middle East Media Research Institute Report* (MEMRI), August 2000, 1815 H Street, NW Suite 404 Washington, DC 20006.

CHAPTER 2

Democracy: Do We Vote for Paul or Plato?

If my grandmother was rooted with the Protestant purity ethic that cleanliness was next to godliness, then I must have grown up with the assumption that democracy held an even more significant corner on the divine than did cleanliness. And since democracy was cleaner than cleanliness, if you didn't swallow it, then you must be some sort of a heretic.

There's only one problem. I've searched the Scriptures from alpha to omega and I have yet to find one text about democracy or human rights. Sorry, I did find one brief text about human rights. It's in Lamentations (just after Jeremiah if you're new at this), right around the middle of Chapter 3.

> *For men are not cast off by the Lord forever. Though he brings grief, he will show compassion, so great is his unfailing love. For he does not willingly bring affliction or grief to the children of men. To crush underfoot all prisoners in the land,* **to deny a man his rights before the Most High,** *to deprive a man of justice—would not the Lord see such things?* (Lamentations 3:31-36)

The emphasis on verse 35 is mine. Every man (and every woman, too) has a divine right to stand before the Most High

for righteous justice. That's it for human rights! The Bible actually gets more into human responsibilities than human rights,
but not everybody gets as excited about that side of the coin.

I recall reading a book some years ago by Mabel
Williamson on the sacrificial challenge of missions titled,
Have We No Right?[1] She dealt with many of the privileges one
gives up in going to a Third World setting which are taken for
granted as rights if not necessities in the homeland. Her
premise was that as bondservants of the King, we really have
no rights at all. If one is into the Scriptures, she is right on,
even though it may seem unjust to most, if not a bit painful.

That's what servanthood is all about, notwithstanding we
have a new set of "high priests" in charge these days with a not-
quite-so-high value system. This enlightened elite have come to
reckon that human rights are, after all, pretty important.

Now, don't get me wrong. No way do I advocate torture,
political oppression, poverty, deprivation of decency or justice,
or any and all other nasty treatment. In fact, I presume to
have as much or more sensitivity to the downtrodden than
most. But if this same crowd would not have chucked out the
Scriptures a few decades back, the world today—or, at least,
much of it—just might have had a better handle on how God
Himself intended for *everyone* to treat his fellowman. And
they wouldn't have to try to rewrite an edict to facilitate the
problem. The worst debacle with the neo-version of just and
fair treatment as outlined in the United Nations Universal
Declaration of Human Rights is that the outworking of it in
most corners of the globe becomes suspiciously selective. All
too often it is targeted to be a cover-up of the guilty—their
"right" to keep off the hook—while the actual victims of society bleed on, internally or otherwise.

Democracy—and the humanist bent—was an endowment

from the Greeks emanating somewhere between the fourth and fifth centuries BC and forward. And as I have already stated, it was most certainly not endorsed by the Bible, not from Moses, Jesus, Paul or anyone else.[2] The Hellenistic mindset created this clever democratic idea as a neat system where everyone gets to have his say. That sounds not too bad for starters—"a fair go" as we'd say down in Aussie land. Ironically, it's the exact antithesis of what Apostle Paul wrote in his letter to the Corinthians:

> *So we fix our eyes not on what is seen, but on what is unseen. For what is seen is temporary, but what is unseen is eternal* (2 Corinthians 4:18).

Obviously, the Greeks didn't like that one so they turned it on its head, and as a result came up with not a few Hellenistic fans in our Western mindset today. You can't see God, but you can see your own hands and we can see each other, so let's get on with it! So much for the origins of humanism. Yet before we go on we might just pause a moment—is your worldview more like Plato's or more like Paul's?[3] Now we can go.

Our Western society has honed democracy to quite a bit more perfection since those ancient times. Some of the big powers have gotten rid of their kings and things like that, and have taken on this conception of individualism and human authority with a vengeance. It worked fairly well for a century or two until some of the splinter interests realized that if you pooled your rights you get more rights, until push comes to shove, and by then political biceps become even more valuable than ordinary votes. A bit of cash within the system—or outside, as the case may be—can do wonders for the results as well. So the power of political leverage is added, and we come up with some very practical—for those at the top, that is—genetically modified constitutional democracy. The dream ends abruptly with a rude awakening for those a bit further down the ladder.

Few would deny, on the other hand, that a smidgen of little America, wherever you may discover it around the globe, is a tad more palatable than the Adolph Hitlers, the Idi Amins, the cruelty of most fanatic Islamic regimes or other butchers of history. No question about that whatsoever. It's just that people power is nowhere near God's primary purposes. And for our purposes, we dare not forget that the good is the enemy of the best.

Winston Churchill, had a pretty good grasp on it when he postulated: "Democracy is the worst form of government there is—except for any other."

Another very poignant article by Yael Amishav Medved appeared in the *Jerusalem Post*:

> Citizens of countries boasting a 'democratic form of government' are becoming increasingly disillusioned with their political system…most are understandably cynical about the 'hard facts' of democracy. Politicians are mostly perceived as self-serving liars and crooks. This is a result of the intolerable gap between the politicians' campaign platforms and their post-election activity. Elected politicians often appear to be furthering their own agendas. Voters feel cheated. Democracy is reduced to a competition between candidates in the art of deceiving the electorate.[4]

Now here's the clue. If justice is manipulated, it's not justice. It's injustice. If democracy is manipulated, it's just sharp politics.

Let's have a look. Most countries don't have compulsory voting. If only 80% of the voters show up, a president or prime minister can get elected on 41% of the vote. If the good citizens are really asleep at the switch and only 50% show up, the young man at the top (read: boy) can waltz in with with the support of a mere one-fourth of the whole clan! And no one even blinks. Never mind. If it is "constitutionally" orchestrated, the box with the big glass eye assures us it must be squeaky clean.

Here's another one from the not too distant memory. Remember this blood thirsty maniac named Milosevic? Who told us he was a maniac? The "democratic" media, of course! How often? Every night for months!

Now I do not personally know the man, but I know quite a few decent, law-abiding Serbs who do. And I did see him join hands and bow his head in prayer with Rev. Jesse Jackson somewhere during the crisis. Now any phony hypocrite can bow his head in prayer for the TV lens, but an accurate assessment is that most of these guys are far too proud to do so, and wouldn't be caught dead in that humble pose, feigned or otherwise.

Regardless, the media, Messrs. Clinton and Blair, and not a few of their pals in NATO daily roasted Milosevic for breakfast. They "democratically" skewered him. Obviously they had the perfect right to do so because the two major leaders had both been elected "democratically." No other votes—according to the logic of the hour—were needed to try the madman.

But why is Mr. Serbia singled out from all the other agents of genocide around the globe? It could hardly have been only because of his alleged violent crimes against those who were seeking to take over Kosovo—the historic heartland of his nation. Our two major protégées of democracy, along with their other European counterparts, seem to have no problem sitting down and chatting with the likes of the late Hafez al Assad of Syria who from 1961 through the 1970s murdered tens of thousands of Syria's minority Kurdish population, and who again in 1982 butchered some 20,000 of his own Syrian civilian population just to keep his "democratic" grasp on power.[5] And even worse was the cozy relationship Mr. Clinton curried with the blood curdling terrorist-cum-comrade, "Adolph" Arafat[6], whose blood soaked terrorist credentials became buried in the archives once he was deemed useful to the king makers. This particular mass murderer made 17 visits to the White House in Clinton's term of office—more than any other legitimate world leader! And all of these men meet regularly with President Putin from Russia as a respected colleague, whose war in Chechnya had and still has a distinct reflection of a very parallel war in Kosovo.

This is not to minimize any alleged crimes of Mr. Milosevic on anyone else who commits mayhem, murder or genocide. Rather it is to underline the hypocrisy of a system that neither came from God, is ordained of God nor represents the even handed justice of the King of the universe.

Moreover, there are two reasons for everything—a *good* reason and the *real* reason. One good reason is that most nations get a bit edgy on the prospect of getting their airliners and World Trade Centers blown up when they happen to pick the wrong side in an international dispute. Could another reason be petrodollars?

As we proceed, could it be that in our day and time, dollars seem to have become the most democratic thing of all?

They even both start with the letter D! Perhaps even the ancient Greeks would begin to get a little nauseated.

I wonder if you have ever noticed that the "great democracies" of our time are brilliant with "tough justice" on the smaller boys in the class until it comes to confrontation of the ominous Islamic sprawl into formerly non-Muslim lands? Once the citizenry bears a partial facade of Islam, their psyche, not to mention that of their mentors, dictates that they must now "claim" their own turf to the demise of the legitimate owners of the land. And the champions of "democracy" and "human rights" always tend to look in the opposite direction at the appropriate moment.

Did you realize that in the beginning the Ancient of Days designated which people groups were to live where? Check out the perception He gave to Moses in instructing the tribes of Israel:

> *When the Most High gave the nations their inheritance, when he divided all mankind, he set up boundaries for the peoples according to the number of the sons of Israel* (Deuteronomy 32.8).

This precept is also reechoed in the New Testament:

> *From one man he made every nation of men, that they should inhabit the whole earth; and he determined the times set for them and the exact places where they should live* (Acts 17:26).[7]

This invites interesting implications for the colonial powers from the 17th century to the present who took upon themselves the mantle of modern real estate re-adjusters. Quite oblivious to linguistic and cultural boundaries, not to mention the divine decree over many millennia of the Almighty's initial distribution of people groups, they redrew lines in sand or sea without the slightest sensitivity to demographic considerations. Today the once colonized but currently "developing" world bears the burden of colonial greed and heartless measures toward people groups quite as human as they. Not infrequently they still pay with their blood for ignorantly carved international boundaries, which not only divide ethnic groups, but also senselessly thrust together former enemies.

Three very vivid instances of this irrational audacity happen to be in my very own arena of service over the last four decades, and I have repeatedly grieved at the disadvantages carelessly unloaded upon these indigenous peoples. Both the indiscriminately drawn borders on the east and west of Papua New Guinea have fostered ethnic wars that have continued to the time of this writing. Likewise, an insensitivity to clan boundaries in the Solomon Islands during World War II ultimately lit the fuse to a bloody civil war, which likewise continues to this day.

Then there is the Middle East where again I have spent much time and research reflecting upon the bizarre lines in the desert, all of which have produced a bountiful harvest of wars and rumors of wars. Let's have a short quiz. Which two prominent Western nations initially set up Saddam Hussein only to turn around to join hands and hardware in an attempt to bomb him into oblivion? To the chagrin of many of his adversaries, they succeeded in the plan but failed in the objective!

But what does this have to do with the demise of democracy? Much, indeed! The very European nations that did so much devastation with their geographical meat cleavers are the identical ones who today are "developing" these Third World nations with a brand of "constitutional democracy" (read: "shifted-foundation" democracy) that neither fits their respective cultures nor has an iota of promise to benefit their masses of poor and underprivileged. It is an appalling exposé of humanistic "blessings" as we shall see even further in Chapter 10.

But there are a few other countries as well that have been blessed by "democratic" intervention, which had not been quite as far down the economic ladder as those several mentioned above. Let's have a look at a few insights into some of the more prominent "democratic" reshuffling of the once divinely distributed "land inheritance deck" of more recent memory.

Bosnia was another glaring "democratic" media job. Who were these people? Some were of Turkish roots who migrated westward centuries ago. Most were Slavic converts to Islam who ultimately demanded that Yugoslavia release ground to afford them their own independent state. With the assistance of the United Nations, the intervention of the West, and an overwhelming media "interpretation" of the Bosnian slant to the story, they eventually achieved their demands.

The Philippines have been fighting Islamic rebels for decades now. Who are they? Filipinos who have become Muslims and as a consequence now demand their own independent turf.

Since the Dutch had previously laid claim to half of New Guinea in their Dutch East Indies colonial empire, when these Malay oriented islands gained their independence from the Dutch in 1949, this newly formed Indonesian Islamic republic proceeded in their ambition to likewise swallow the ethnically diverse, pro-Christian West New Guinea in 1963. The Melanesians from West New Guinea have chaffed and bled under the burden of their Islamic oppressors ever since. But to date, rescue efforts either by stealth bombers or even by UN economic sanctions are nowhere on the horizon. Interesting, this global humanitarian justice!

Islamic Sudan has butchered, starved and enslaved the Christian south with nary a blink from the "democratic" protectors of the downtrodden and the exploited. The sacrificial efforts of decades of service by the Sudan Interior Mission has been systematically shattered with blatant genocide. The great powers of the West refuse to intervene.

Finally, the duplicity of the century—the 20th century, that is, with no respite in sight—is that the Islamic-cum-Palestinian combo somehow has a legitimate claim to the land of Israel. The land lay desolate of population for centuries. In particular, reports published during the latter half of the 19th century specifically noted the phenomenon of extremely sparse population.[8] The Jews began their long-awaited journey back to their ancient homeland around the turn of the century, and their Arab cousins began to follow them shortly thereafter. According to UK demographic statistics, the majority of Arabs migrated to Israel primarily after World War I under the British mandate, but Palestinian propaganda experts have limited use for authentic historical records.[9]

Now if you're into Darwin or relegate the pages of Scripture to some archaic age of Hebraic dreamers, most of this probably won't bother you too much. But let's back off for a bit of evaluation and reflect for just a moment. This book is not a political treatise. Rather, it's about what God gave us in the Bible. It's about a divinely ordained dominion of justice, righteousness and ultimate judgment. We have been immersed into the principle that the separation of church and state is bedrock and inviolable. I certainly have no problems with that. It has had disastrous effects in the past. But to separate God and state? Now there's the problem! In too many circumstances the church has presumed herself to be God Himself, and, unfortunately, few there be in the real world who know the difference!

Political shenanigans must be exposed front and center stage because—as we shall see—the humanistic political scenario most certainly will be the Almighty's most highly charged opponent in the final countdown.

It shouldn't take the brilliance of a brain surgeon to recognize that the first-born son of democracy is human rights, and the ultimate grandson is anarchy. If you question this, you might just have a look around you. The legality of God's justice was reflected in Mosaic precepts and was the bedrock upon which the legal systems of most Western nations were initially founded. No longer. The divine principles of the Almighty have long been pared away and replaced with humanistic-oriented legislation. The shiny, new trophy on the mantle is litigation. Punishing the guilty is out—far out. He has his rights, you know. Cashing in on big bucks is in.

Through the politically sanctified promotion of human rights, we now have inherited a value system which is totally across the compass from the Judeo-Christian tradition. True justice, on the other hand, leaps directly out of the Bible. It is the resounding theme of the Old Testament (really, there's nothing old about it—I prefer calling it the Foundational Testament), and it is repeatedly echoed by Jesus in the New. Authentic justice is God's divine address, while mercy is His telephone number.[10]

And to verify the declared standard of His bottom line:

Your throne, O God, will last for ever and ever; a scepter of justice will be the scepter of your kingdom (Psalm 45:6).

God gave Moses and the offspring of Israel the divine concepts of His accuracy—let's call it His righteousness, His justice and a legal system that blended these two into a prescription for positive human relationships to last forever and a day. Nor was it meant just for Jews. According to the promise to Abraham and the patriarchs, it was a divine plan— a blessing, in fact—for the whole world, including all humankind yet to be born.

Then humanity hit a problem or two. The Israelites who were meant to pick up the ball and run with it, didn't always take too kindly to God snooping around in their affairs. You can read some about this in the Scriptures, which give realistic, un-fudged reports of not a few of their somewhat shabby kings and shady stand-ins. And the Almighty did, indeed, take issue with the rebellious ones from time to time, administering a tad of divine chastisement.

Then came the diabolic hiccup. As we have already discussed, Greek thinking hit the world market, and what was to become known as the Western world bought into it. In the briefest of terms, Hellenism shifted the concept of a God-ordained global family[11] living in harmony with their Abba[12] to a focus on—and preeminence of—the individual. Humanism and human rights were thus spawned for an eventual head-on showdown with the alternative agenda of a Creator God.

Over the last decade or so, however, many of God's people have been awakening to the fact of just how much New Age reasoning had crept into their (and our) worldview over the intervening years without ever having realized it. It is not in my purpose here to further expand on the wide discrepancies existing between the two competing systems, but research and publication already done on the vast spiritual gulf between God's initially programmed Hebraic order versus the opposing Hellenistic worldview will adequately satisfy the interest of those who want to pursue it.[13]

1 Mabel Williamson, *Have We No Right?* (London: China Inland Mission; Lutterworth Press, 1958).

2 The concept, however, does have a negative reference in the Scriptures in Judges 21:25.

3 See Christian Overman, *Assumptions that Affect Our Lives* (Simi Valley, CA: Micah 6:8 Publishers); "The Problem with Plato's Dualism" and "Tracing Plato through the Church," pp. 155-169; and "The Influence of Aristotle on Western Civilzation," pp.170-175.

4 "Can Democracy Be Saved From the Politicians?" by Yael Amishav Medved, *Jerusalem Post,* OP-ED, Sept. 20, 2000.

5 Netanyahu, op. cit. pp. 98-99.

6 The world dare not overlook the diabolical sequence of attempts on the ultimate elimination of world Jewry by the schemes of the "Pharoahs" and "Hamans" throughout history down to Adolph Hitler and, currently, Yasser Arafat and the fundamentalist terrorist organizations aligned with him.

7 A concept further reiterated in Ps. 74:17 and Job 12:23.

8 Mark Twain, *The Innocents Abroad* (New York: Literary Classics of the United States, 1984), pp. 349, 441-442; Peters, op. cit. pp. 157-161.

9 Barry Chamish, *The Last Days of Israel: "*Why the Palestinians Have No Right to a State" (Tempe, AZ: Dandelion Books, 2001), pp. 112-114. Also see Peters, op. cit. Chapter 12 "A Hidden Factor in Western Palestine: Arab Immigration," pp. 234-268 and Chapter 13 "A Hidden Movement: Illegal Arab Immigration," pp. 269-295.

10 Those who unwittingly hold a stereotype of an Old Testament that reflects only God's wrath while assuming the New Testament counters with His mercy will benefit from additional in-depth study. Also for a good telephone number, try PSA-5115 or, less cryptically, Psalm 51:15a.

11 Genesis 12:3.

12 Abba is the intimate Hebrew word for father. See Mark 14:36, Rom. 8:15b and Gal. 4:6.

13 An extraordinary text is Christian Overman, *Assumptions That Affect Our Lives* (Simi Valley, CA: Micah 6:8 Publishers); specifically "The Difference Between Greek and Hebrew Thought," pp. 21-35; "The Problem With Plato's Dualism" and "Tracing Plato through the Church," pp. 155-169; and "The Influence of Aristotle on Western Civilzation," pp.170-175. Overman's website is also accessible on: www.biblical-worldview.com. See also Jerusalem Perspective: www.jerusalemperspective.com and Dr. Garr Restoration Foundation Website: www.restorationfoundation.org or *Restore,* (Atlanta, GA. 1995-2001), researching Hebraic roots, reflection and insights.

CHAPTER 3

Will the Global Village
Need a Big Jail?

It would be difficult to know for sure if she was the one who initially coined the phrase, but she certainly promoted it's popularity. Dame Hillary Clinton, BTS (standing for "Before the Senate," a miserable effort of mine to maneuver some sort of royal status for Americans) reflects a glowing messianic-like yearning for a Global Village where all the children could play in blissful harmony. Who wouldn't hope for that?

Ironically, Someone else gave us indication of the same kind of an idea eons ago. His version, however, sounded more like a "Now-It's-My-Turn City" than a Phoenixville evolving from erstwhile political ashes. His rendition even promised streets of gold, which to the mature mind rings too much like fantasy—more tinny than gold perhaps—and sets it quite out of any realistic reach for a world come-of-age. However, since the Ancient of Days does seem to hold a fair edge in experience, as well as an impressive tenure on truth, I, for one, opt for His previously proposed model. Neither experience nor truth are in the greatest of supply these days!

Yet, on the other hand, Hillary's dream-town has a bit of a humble ring, like catering to the needs of the young and innocent. And, to be fair, her focus was primarily on the playground of that cozy little village-oriented globe with all the kids doing the right things, loving each other, helping each other, deferring to one another, patting all the other children on the back, gently with open palms and not with sharp knives! I mean, that sounds fantastic.

Nevertheless, whether for Hillary's playground or for anyone else's expanded ideas for City Hall, I see a few red lights flashing in Dreamville, for whatever agenda might be visualized—or perhaps schemed. For example, will these visions of the day bode as well for New Delhi as for New York? And is even the kaleidoscope of New York a sane assumption for modeling ecstasy (the legal kind)?

There's a couple of worrisome details not yet announced, like, who will be the mayor? Perhaps "constitutional democracy" as is currently being exported across the planet will deal with that one. But, of course, that also gets a bit scary as we have taken note in the preceding chapter.

There's yet another problem—quite probably of more major proportions than the one above. We earthlings have never taken too willingly to concepts of kindness, sharing, selflessness and back patting (without sharp blades, that is). Who is going to help us adjust these minor social and moral details? The noble village, it seems, will require a very tough constable with plenty of husky helpers, not to mention a goodly supply of closed circuit TV cameras. George Orwell's mid-20th century allegorical predictions of these days become chillingly relevant![1]

On the other hand, the days may not be too far around the corner where some would even welcome this respite of repressive sovereignty in contrast to the chaos which predictably may well be erupting over on the other side of town. Not long ago *Time Magazine* published a most perceptive article on this very evolution of globalization, noting that with the easing of international tensions, "fewer and fewer wars take place these days *across* these (international) borders, and more and more take place *within* them."[2] Hopefully, the town planners have thought of all these details, but with the politicians, you never know.

Getting even more serious, IF there happens to be NO sovereign God Almighty of biblical renown, IF there is no real God of Abraham, Isaac and Jacob, and IF there is no down-to-earth Abba of a Yeshua who referred to Himself as the Son of Man, then the global visionaries have possibly set their hopes on the next best option. May I suggest that with our planet currently coming apart socially, spiritually, morally, economically and environmentally, like fourth generation hand-me-down furniture, the future is not looking all that flash. So it's either the Global Village that comes to the rescue, or an eternal God who said what He meant and meant what He said. There's not much else on the horizon!

Unfortunately, great masses in Europe, Australia, Canada and New Zealand would tend to agree with the understanding that the archaic idea of a concerned and caring God has quite run out of steam. Mistaking organized religion for spirituality, and church fidelity for faith, the masses of the disillusioned multitudes have clearly dropped the ball. They have recognized that religious systems as a solution are less than helpful; "religion" as it is perceived, neither "scratches where it itches" nor delivers fulfillment to an emptiness of the soul. So, why bother?

America is a bit different. A belief in God is still well over 50%. Unfortunately—and here I want to be totally honest, but hardly offensive—too much of America's view of God has a "Made in USA" label on it. Europe and the rest of the world see this quite clearly, and as a result have never totally tuned in to this less than understood populist presentation of the Almighty.

One interesting awakening of late—and that from all quarters of the globe—is that over the last few decades, many of the faithful from around the world have begun to notice that the stamp on the original "product" was, after all, "Made in Israel"; notwithstanding, an export license has been duly secured for all nations. But for actual achievement, no country or creed from east or west, north or south, dare lay any claim for superior nationalistic performance. That, of course, includes America and Israel as well.

Having said that, however, with regard to a renewed awakening, there have been interesting movements in the Third World quite at the periphery of any hard and fast organized religious systems. These are primarily in nations from the far less developed Southern Hemisphere, which has been stirring to a much wider recognition of the reality of a creator God. The secular West may charitably overlook this naïve expression of faith of these "less complicated" societies—if, indeed, it notices their sincerity at all—as intellectual immaturity which will fade as new global markets (read: materialism) are generated. This may well be true for some, but for the others of the newly responding, let us wait and see what their Abba will ultimately do.

Finally, in yet another massive international distribution of humankind, there are approximately 1.2 billion Muslims stretching from the Philippines and the Indonesian archipelago in the Pacific region, circumscribing nearly half the globe to the West African nations of Morocco and Mauritania bordering on the Atlantic. And of utmost significance, I am sure you must be aware of the long standing Islamic boycott for any and all products that even hint of Israel. Heading that list without question is the Judeo-Christian God whom we first meet in the Hebrew Scriptures. With regard to a deity, they have developed their own far "superior" model out of Mecca, and the sales competition is—shall we say—cutthroat to the bitter end.

So how can these minor wrinkles be ironed out for said Global Village? Fences? They haven't worked so far! If any concept of a Global Village is ever to get off the ground sufficiently, they are going to have to come up with a new candidate for "number one" altogether. And that new god on the global block can be none other than our sometime friend, "constitutional democracy." And its messianic message is global trade!

Moreover, the services of Moses the lawgiver, whose divine records were the basis for almost all Western systems of legality up to about four decades ago, happen to be no longer needed in drawing up the new constitution. But this time around, they are going to be fair to *everyone*, and especially to those who didn't like the Almighty's first round of precepts. Most other religions—as the world systems understand religion—will be able to nicely accommodate their new boss since politics, economics and greed rarely interfere with innocuous closed-door rites and ceremonies. On the other hand, when absolutes, morals and any alternative authority begins poking its nose into presumed government business, then we've got problems.

Perhaps at this juncture, it should again be underlined that what most mortals understand as "religion" is a far cry from a realistic relationship with the Lord of life, and it is never, ever guaranteed that the twain shall somehow meet.

In this same vein, the most highly renowned Jew who ever lived taught with authority that one cannot serve both God (whom He called Abba) and mammon.³ Some of our better theological thinkers these days, reckon that this certainly must have been only a suggestion at best, or perhaps even a misprint! On the other hand, if after all, that's what He really said, and if in a final showdown of priorities, appetites and other little greedy ambitions, Mr. Mammon happens to get himself elected as the Chairman of the Board of the New Village Development Society, guess who has to leave town. Not only the one who gave mammon thumbs down, but His Abba, as well, who thundered with divine proclamation from Mount Sinai, "You shall have no other gods before me."⁴

Well, if there is no such God, never was such a God or if He spun His top somewhere between Mars and Venus and then went off to play with other celestial toys, perhaps the global thinkers are on the right track. Benign ritual can stay; absolutes including the only Absolute of the ages must go. But if the Most High is exactly what His title declares Him to be, perhaps it's time to wake up and notice what's going on in the streets below.

This Global Village scenario is hardly new. I suggest we read up on the first try in Genesis 11 on the plain of Shinar, later called Babel because of a slight linguistic hiccup somewhere during construction time. I know you know that old story called "The Tower of Babel":

> As men moved eastward, they found a plain in Shinar and settled there. They said to each other, "Come, let's make bricks and bake them thoroughly."... They said, "Come, let us build ourselves a city, with a tower that reaches to the heavens, so that we may make a name for ourselves and not be scattered over the face of the whole earth." But the LORD came down to see the city and the tower that the

men were building. The LORD said, "If as one people speaking the same language they have begun to do this, then nothing they plan to do will be impossible for them" (Genesis 11:2-6).

I hope we're clear that the King of the Universe has no major problems with tall buildings. That's not quite the point. The sum and substance of the structure touching heaven was hardly the physical height, but rather the political intent—playing God, doing it better than He can—upstaging the Ancient of Days. The eternal pursuit of mankind competing with his creator has forever been to erect a society that can do nicely on its own without that frustrating interference from Above!

The Tower of Babel was the initial attempt, a type of our currently contemplated Global Village where His services will no longer be needed—thank you very much!

Predictably (that is, for those who know Him well enough to also call Him Abba), He cut the infamous construction project off, and it fell flat before it figuratively got off to cloud one. Reflecting on the flop of this precarious forerunner of our presently proposed Village, might we instead nickname our sought after 21st century version the Leaning Tower of Pizza?

No, that's not a typo. The popular but otherwise quite ordinary dish from Italy has spread throughout the Western world. It will more than serve our purposes to point to a middle-of-the-road affluence that few of the masses of the developing world have yet to taste, while at the same time, link this unlikely symbol to the clichéd shaky structure of Pisa, whose name ironically enhances the scene. The law of gravity revisited! What goes up in faulty fashion will surely take a more direct route down. A globe of unjust imbalance is doomed for cataclysmic crash.

But just a minute. Plain old pizza—a symbol of affluence? Affluence, indeed! And since we are already supplied with a sound-alike tower, I tell you, it's not really a bad word picture.

The architects of globalism are an elite minority wedded to a Western world whose banker may be City Bank of New York or perhaps Chase Manhattan, whose financier is probably on Wall Street, whose insurer may well be Lloyds of London, and whose right arm embraces the International Monetary Fund. These powerful ones—along with most of the rest of us "ordinary creatures" who unwittingly bask in their shadow— have never walked alongside the crushed and destitute 80% of the earth's poorest. Much less do those mighty ones—nor even most of the lesser ones among us who presume middle ground—have the capacity to truly empathize with the impoverished billions whose mere existence is a struggle to survive.

The dubious link of these struggling masses with the power brokers of World Bank status is an artificially groomed colonial-type elite who themselves are millionaires compared to their subsistence-oriented subordinates strewn from the less than glorious bush to the borderless squalor of festering urban slums. Their daily indulgence is rice or beans, taro or sago, while their more privileged seaside dwellers might yet add a fish or coconut to the sameness of yesterday. But at least they eat. Yet to these, our symbolic affluence of pizza is an unheard of luxury, and the precarious globally imbalanced tower of some 20% haves and the rest have-nots will not keep leaning forever!

Unfortunately, the oh-so-happy idealism of a Global Village is naïve at best, and a cynical maneuver by carefree dreamers at worst.

I certainly do not want to be hard on the honest efforts of the countless among the concerned who try to help the hurting as best they know how. The problem is that the actual "know-how" is in all too short supply. There was an insightful publication some years ago promoted by the Wycliffe Bible Translators titled, *It Takes Time to Love*.[5] Philanthropy cannot be accomplished by money alone, like tossing even a sizable note into the beggar's bowl. Like feeding animals at a zoo—which is most often forbidden anyway since the benefactors usually don't have a clue what sort of junk they are handing out—it's the givers who actually get the jollies, and the poor creatures who cop the bellyache. It truly does take time to love—to voluntarily become a part of the pain.[6]

In a report called the "Real Global Village," Zachary Pascal[7] tells of a hideaway rain forest village in Borneo that was anticipating their first electric power line and perhaps even a village telephone, which would inevitably transform their lives forever and a day. And he makes a more than valid observation that Western technical innovations must be adapted both in their own filter of understanding and in their own cultural way. Indeed! Unfortunately, he was visiting the village at the beginning of the dream. I have been an observer of innumerable parallel projects to see the other end of the "development"—the shattered dream!

I'll never forget the massive overhead surgical light to illuminate the operating table in a small but once impressive hospital in West Ambai in the Republic of Vanuatu. West Ambai, incidentally, was the tiny New Hebrides island where the box office giant of its day, *South Pacific*, had been once filmed. The cast was long gone. So was the electric power. Dust covered the expensive lighting fixture and the now rusting surgical instruments along with everything else in the once sterile operating room. The windows were broken and doors of the hospital were closed. Like in a myriad of similar settings throughout the developing world, there were no actors left to act!

In our long-term tenure in Papua New Guinea, I can well remember the early years of the note-in-the-bottle type of overseas snail communication. Then came development. What incredible progress! Telephones finally came to Mendi, the Provincial Center of the Southern Highlands. Some years later the technology so blossomed that the government outposts, the trading companies, the churches and even a few private politicians had their own telephones. What ultimate bliss!

Then came the dark side of the moon. The children of extortion, the offspring of litigation, and the descendants of greed were conceived. And these kids grew up. Many had a high school education—even some had university—obvious add-on blessings from Western philanthropy and global assistance packages. One special treat were those violent videos also from the West to add to their moral and spiritual insights! And, of course, there were no jobs. Too many politicians had all that big development money in their pockets—if not in offshore investments.

So the kids started dreaming up their own "business ventures," the easiest startup kit being a large bush knife for the purpose of armed highway holdups after duly blocking a vulnerable section of the road. Police? Once in a while! Notwithstanding, this has become a relatively widespread fact of life.

If the boys really want to avoid the cops, they have taken note that it is impossible to protect those solar panels high on the isolated mountaintops, which have made Telecom hum so beautifully during those few "developed" years. So down come the solar panels for village home lighting purposes and out go hundreds of rural telephones. Even the police buy a panel or two at times, as well as an occasional church pastor who cannot detect any moral difference in this shenanigan from many of the other shady standards exported from the West! We remember, of course, that the Western world had long jettisoned Moses who was a tad intransigent on stealing, and brought in some much improved legislation that affords license to certain appetites within the society. Need it be said that this makes it quite confusing for those unskilled in sorting out the legal loopholes for the elite.

Moreover, in the course of time, the innovations of the left-outs become more creative and their illicit trade more brisk. Along with a bush technology, they glean their moral and ethical cues from film producers abroad to team up for an unseemly "development" scheme fusing the violent video titans with the falcons of the bush. But perhaps the most woeful note is that due to lack of technical expertise, some of the stolen panels may never ever find their way to even a minimal usage to benefit a few unwitting villagers, who, knowing nothing of the crime or the enormous waste, remain quite in the dark about the whole debacle! And all the while, communication in the Southern Highlands is back to a simulated relay race in the Snail Olympics.

Yes indeed, it takes time to love, and neither the big bucks nor the multinationals will ever fill the chasm. Been there—seen that!

In fact, I've seen too much of it. I could tell you endless tales of ruined roads, literal and otherwise, paved with the best of intentions all leading to destruction. It's utterly disheartening to survey the rotting classrooms, empty stores, non-existent government services and deteriorating clinic buildings whose grimy shelves contain not even an aspirin. Those

Global Village experts are going to have to do a lot more homework—including a survey of the whole sordid mess with the same lenses that Abba uses, and then to eventually understand what it means to love one's neighbor.

Forty years of my life have been in the grassroots—not to mention mud—of the Third World. I know it intimately. The rich are getting richer and the poor are getting more desperately destitute. The International Monetary Fund's programs and World Bank Funding, notwithstanding, we see little more than developmental window dressing to the nations that are hurting the most. In fact, these very institutions may well be a major contributor to the problem as we shall see in a later chapter.

In a graphic picture of reality—worth 10,000 words at least—Dr. Phillip M. Harter, on the medical staff of Stanford University School of Medicine in California, made some fascinating calculations that give a jarring awakening. An abridged list of Dr. Harter's statistics bear witness to what he entitles "The Fortunate Few":

If earth's population were shrunk into a village of just 100 people—with all the human ratios existing in the world still remaining—what would this tiny, diverse village look like?

57 would be Asian
21 would be European
14 would be from the Western Hemisphere
 8 would be African
70 would be non-white
30 would be white
70 would be non-Christian
30 would be Christian

6 would possess 59 percent of the entire world's wealth,
    and all 6 would be from the United States
80 would live in substandard housing
70 would be unable to read
50 would suffer from malnutrition...
  1 would have a college education
  1 would own a computer.

So to wind up on a retry at Babel, our tongue-in-cheek terminology of a Leaning Tower of Pizza is probably apropos. Its pretty certain that the latest version of Babelville will likewise never make it to intercept the heavenlies. If we can believe the Old Testament—the Foundational Scriptures for all the King of Creation says and does thereafter—His two bedrock principles are righteousness and justice for everyone, neither of which seems to be a recognized priority for Godfree City. If over half the town can't even get a whiff of the affluence of a minority elite, for example, there are some frightening structural cracks in the foundation. It ain't gonna fly very high!

Beyond the glaring gulf between the haves and have-nots in Dr. Harter's calculations—which from world economic trends can only widen in McVillage—I would like to add a couple of my own computations to his statistics. May I point out that 17 in the village would be Muslim, but—with the worldwide Jewry numbering but two-tenths of one percent of the entire world population—by proportional representation, there would be nary a Jew in town. Very interesting!

Of course, this is but a ratio on the basis of 100 total, while the projected numbers for the City of Gold is in the multitudes, and surely is the one and only venue in the universe where one can be absolutely certain of no *Judenrein*.[8]

But my observation is, rather, how minute is the population of world Jewry in proportion to the overwhelming flood of Gentiles! Which leads to the next question.

Ever wonder why the Jew is despised so much by the Islamic world-at-large? This is not to mention their disdain by the secular international media, and to a large degree most member states in the United Nations? And why are all those tombstone desecrating, synagogue torching, Holocaust denying anti-Semites found the world over? Our above statistics must tell us loud and clear that it certainly isn't because of the Jews' ominously threatening numbers worldwide! It could be their notable achievements, such as, while the Jews number but 0.2% of the world's population, they merit roughly 10% of the world's Nobel prizes in Science and Medicine. But such an intense hatred generated for that simple achievement really doesn't make sense either.

It couldn't be that underneath the surface they don't like the Jews' Abba, could it?

---

1 See George Orwell, *1984* (Canada: Penguin Books, Ltd., 1976).

2 "Are We Coming Apart or Together?" by Pico Iyer, *Time*, May 22, 2000.

3 Matthew 6:24 (KJV), Luke 16:13 (KJV)

4 Exodus 20:3.

5 Hugh Steven, *It Takes Time to Love* (Glendale, CA: Church Press, 1974).

6 See also William J. Lederer & Eugene Burdick's classic: *The Ugly American* (Paperback: WW Norton & Co, 1998).

7 "The Real Global Village" by Zachary G. Pascal, *Technology Review*, July-August, 1999.

8 Literally in German, "Free of Jews," as routinely and blatantly mandated throughout Nazi Germany and much of anti-Semitic Europe, coming to its eventual diabolic intensity in the late 1930s and into the Holocaust of World War II.

CHAPTER 4
Lies and Rumors of Lies

The celebrated Mark Twain made the classic observation that if you don't read the newspaper you're uninformed—if you do read it, you're misinformed. That was well over a century ago!

So what has changed? Not much, and certainly not for the better. That was before radio and before the magic box with the twinkle in its eye that has wasted more time, enslaved more people, stifled more creativity and cloned more disciples of mesmerized mentality than any other shoehorn since the beginning of time. The shoehorn gets the less than creative into the booby box, and there they vegetate, rarely to emerge again with any positive insights of their own. All we dare expect is a warmed over army of mediocre thinkers, prepared by a microwave designed especially for Hollywood brain waves. And, alas, a barrier for brilliance is forever fixed.

Sorry, I should back off just a tad. I must admit that we ought to at least try to search for something good in everything. I think it was again Mark Twain who said that there is nothing that does not have some positive value—but the housefly comes close!

So I just remembered that there are two very worthwhile things about those nice nature documentaries. First, they are a positive brain stimulus—a challenge to develop one's own personal intelligence, to try to figure out how in the world they ever get those neat pictures of the lion's tonsils, and, second you do learn a lot about animals, which the disciples of Darwin tell us that God really didn't design after all. Actually, it might be suggested to the gullible that they found some microbe eggs in Galaxy 679-Q, readjusted the DNA repeatedly in a laboratory somewhere in California, and now we can appreciate all these nice creatures. Of course, that's not really true nor even what they tell us (so far), but it does make as much sense. Yet those animals are quite educational to see, and, for myself, I know who actually made them anyway. So there are a few positive values from the box.

Nor is this to say that a smidgen of high quality moral seasoning is never stirred into the soup, but at the end of the day, the diet is still junk food, and the multitudes remain malnourished and sick.

But all this other fiction fodder, this vacuum of the mind, this stifling of creativity for which we were designed is bad enough. Yet there is an equal if not even greater devastation in the perceptions we are methodically given via a "political correctness" legislated by only a minute minority of derelict opinion. Theirs is the diabolical intent to lead the easily influenced masses down a garden path to a tree of knowledge that we can quite well do without. Political correctness is hardly new:

> These are rebellious people, deceitful children…unwilling to listen to the LORD's instruction. They say…to the prophets, "Give us no more visions of what is right! Tell us pleasant things, prophesy illusions. Leave this way, get off this path, and stop confronting us with the Holy One of Israel" (Isaiah 30:9-11).

But I reserve my most pointed indictment specifically for the international news media, to challenge the lies we are systematically told and the innuendoes we are deceptively led to believe. Before we deal with the media on its own, however, are they, in fact, part of a wider collaboration out there for ultimate universal control?

Which in turn leads us to the bottom line question. Is there indeed a planning and plotting takeover crowd lurking somewhere behind the bushes? Although conspiracy theories abound, I actually doubt it. At least, not a humanly ordered conspiracy with conniving secrecy—blinds drawn, doors barred and that sort of thing. You may have noticed by now, that if I can't reference my conclusion in the Scriptures, I dare not get too resolute about it. So how about this one:

> *Do not call conspiracy everything that these people call conspiracy; do not fear what they fear, and do not dread it. The LORD Almighty is the one you are to regard as holy, he is the one you are to fear, he is the one you are to dread, and he will be a sanctuary...* (Isaiah 8:12-14a).

It would appear to me that the kind of worldwide conspiracy that seems to prevail these days is a cocktail of humanistic hatred, greed, intense competition, insatiable sensuality, unlimited indulgence, a lust for the limelight and a lust for power.

The above chain of perversions may frequently link the strangest of bedfellows, and thus gives a semblance of conspiracy, until, of course, the usefulness of one player in the combo fails to satisfy the expectations of the other and the how-can-I-best-use-you game is all over. This is not unlike many marriages these days. Of a certainty, all of these sordid appetites quite respond to the beat of the same drummer—again giving the aura of a conspiracy—though the individual marchers themselves, most likely would not even be aware of which one of Lucifer's little lackeys it is that pipes the tune.

So let's reflect a moment on the conspiracy roster in Paul's letter to young Timothy:

> *But mark this: There will be terrible times in the last days. People will be lovers of themselves, lovers of money, boastful, proud, abusive, disobedient to their parents, ungrateful, unholy, without love, unforgiving, slanderous, without self-control, brutal, not lovers of the good, treacherous, rash, conceited, lovers of pleasure rather than lovers of God—having a form of godliness but denying its power. Have nothing to do with them* (2 Timothy 3:1-5).

Sound familiar? Just refocus the terminology a tad to adapt to our local 21st century scene—domestic, community or political—and we're right at home on Main Street! Herein we have a *bona fide* exposure of who these real "conspirators" are. They are entities, we will note, with neither human names nor human faces. But do they indeed have a chairman of the board out there somewhere?

Apostle Paul jotted this sinister list down a fair few years ago and obviously there's been a slight hiatus of nearly 2000 years. But it has taken until today's demise to put it all together and package it up for a predominately Ichabod generation for whom the glory of God has departed.[1]

Now back to zero in on the media. Since there is such a hard and fast media consensus on who is guilty and who is not, what is just and what is unjust, what is politically correct and what is not, whose "human rights" have priority and whose

43

don't count, is there a sinister connivance going on here? Of course, if we may have presumed that since they all make precisely the same pronouncements, these moguls are all telling us the truth, then we are in deep trouble! So when do these guys get their heads together? Where do they meet? Again, who is the boss in the big seat?

At this point, we will do well to note the savage competition and greed among the media magnates from newsprint conglomerates to digital relay systems, who grapple for boardroom control with obviously little love lost among any of their rival electronic gladiators. Do they have a singular supervisor as they bite and claw, plot and plan to outbid one another in their personal orbit to glory, honor and power? Not likely!

So who's the boss of the whole bit? I think by now you should be able to figure it out. Would you buy a used car from this prince of the demons? Unfortunately, waves of humanity have purchased far too much already and are well past the point of no return. As we check our bearings from the stark arrow in the global mall of human destiny, "YOU ARE HERE." Fortunately, I do note an exit just over there. Can you see it? If you can't, just stick with me for a few more chapters, and I'll take you across myself.

One thing is sure. The media is one of the netherworld's most unconventional weapons, and the big boss hates Abba! Please be awakened. In Revelation 13 there's an interesting side feature in the description of the dreadfully horrifying beast that surfaces out of the sea to overwhelm the masses at the end of days.

> *The beast was given a mouth to utter proud words and blasphemies and to exercise his authority for forty-two months. He opened his mouth to blaspheme God, and to*

slander his name and his dwelling place and those who live in heaven (Revelation 13:5-6).

First of all, let us not get hung up with the 42 months and up to 88 reasons what it might mean. Obviously it does have significant meaning, but not exactly for self-styled prophets to play guessing games. Nevertheless, my purpose at the moment is to focus on the international media at-large and not date-lines.

Thus, my major attention to the text is to take a little survey to check up on whether anyone else seems to sense an interesting connection between the mouth given to this rapacious beast at the end of days and the uncanny capacity of our present-day worldwide news media coverage to undermine truth in any and every form, and to vilify the current countdown agenda of the Most High? Mind you, with regard to a "personified" beast, I am in no way making the slightest innuendo to any media personality whatsoever. But since there are those who think in these terms, I deem it necessary to mention it. This is not a human entity. My thrust here is to recognize this godless shroud of satanic media deception that currently darkens our generation and to ponder the response we must make.

In the prophecy quoted above, we have an horrific beast coming out of the sea whose mouth will thunder an awesome, intimidating and deceitful voice at the end of days. His diabolical design is to defy any and all remaining vestiges of a creator God, to manipulate His truth, to challenge His authority and assume final superiority in anything and everything that is of essence. That sounds uncomfortably close to the news media I encounter daily, which is saturating the globe with its own agenda—lies and rumors of lies!

Lets have a look at a few of the specifics.

Beyond product information and society's sentiments of what is in and what is out, what is cool and what is flaming hot, what is politically correct and which value systems are no longer true—the abominations proliferated by the nightly news media are the most damning of deceptions. Innumerable multitudes of the unsuspecting are molded into the preconceived thought patterns of the mighty. The result is that innocent victims are crushed by the miserable reporting of a minority clique.

ABC anchor Peter Jennings once proclaimed unabashedly, "There is no truth…only news."[2] This is to acknowledge that the news, as reported by the whim of those who select what and what not to report, is basically propaganda. But as Mark Twain cleverly reminded us in our opening lines of this chapter, if you don't monitor the news, you don't know what lies they are feeding to the masses around you, and, in fact, to the whole rest of the world. One of the supporting pillars in a democracy is the freedom of speech, but we need to remind ourselves that the "unfettered freedom of expression includes the freedom to lie."[3] So as we ponder this all-powerful beguiling potentate of our time, what else is new?

Nor is the news any longer "reported." It's interpreted—interpreted according to the impulse, the fantasy, or the worldview of the journalist, cameraman and anchorman or woman doing the reporting. Should unadulterated democracy even be the rule of the day? Who is electing this crowd anyway? These are the all-powerful ones, the ones who tell us one and all what to think, and those who also maintain a massive leverage on politicians and international decisions. They are the "godlings" who now tell the planet what is true and what is false. These are the judges of the highest court in the universe who now rule on who are the good guys and who are the vile ones. But then there is also another most disturbing observation. This electronic judicial bench seems to be quite inaccessible—to the ordinary souls, at least—for any type of appeal for the causes so falsely and corruptly adjudicated!

But we have been forewarned:

Woe to those who draw sin along with cords of deceit, and wickedness as with cart ropes.... Woe to those who call evil good and good evil, who put darkness for light and light for darkness, who put bitter for sweet and sweet for bitter. Woe to those who are wise in their own eyes and clever in their own sight (Isaiah 5:18-21).

On August 17, 1980, Pastor Michael Chamberlain and his wife Lindy were on a family camp-out at magnificent Ayres Rock in outback Australia with their three children, including tiny nine-week-old Azaria. In the early evening, Lindy briefly left a barbecue with fellow campers to return to her tent to change her clothes, as the air had become cool. Within minutes, dire screams from the mother signaled panic. Infant Azaria had mysteriously disappeared from her cot. Her little body was never found. There had been semi-domesticated dingoes—the Australian feral wolf-dog—observed around the periphery of the campsite foraging for bits of food scraps from the campers, and Lindy Chamberlain frantically maintained that one of the dingoes must have snatched baby Azaria and dragged her off into the wilds.

A frenzied, but unfortunately, unprofessional and disorganized night search began. Dingo tracks were found and followed, but there was never a trace of the infant's tiny body.

Some days later, part of Azaria's tattered clothes were discovered near a dingo den some two kilometers from the campsite. However, the little matinee jacket she was wearing was not among them.

But the media was far too clever for that. They projected an Agatha Christie type scenario that the mother herself actually murdered the infant for "child sacrifice," hid the body in the trunk of their car until it could be disposed of, and then clandestinely "planted" the clothes near the dingo den at a later opportunity.

The Chamberlains, it so happened, were devout Seventh Day Adventists, which the crafty secular journalists reflected as a weird, if not dangerous, cult. An uncomfortable number of the investigating police seemed to not only agree but to add their own fuel to the flames. Theories of child sacrifice and ritual murder abounded, which the *Northern Territory News* and the electronic media was quick to amplify across Australia. Then forensic tests detected dried blood in the Chamberlain car. The Chamberlains maintained any blood must have come from a hitchhiker, to whom they had given a ride a few weeks before, whose leg had been bleeding from a roadside injury.

Then more "fetal" blood was found, which all of Australia was given to believe was the most damning evidence yet against Lindy Chamberlain. (It was much later discovered that faulty laboratory reagents erroneously indicated that the protective rust coating on the car floor tested out as "fetal blood.") After more weeks of tests and counter tests, bizarre prosecution charges, questionable police performance and unabated media hype—during all of which the Chamberlains declared injustice, press and police bias, and their innocence throughout— the infallible media won the day. The jury in a "fair and democratic" trial declared Lindy Chamberlain guilty of first-degree murder. She was sentenced to life imprisonment![4]

Lindy Chamberlain anguished in disbelief that fate could have used her so cruelly. Then after three years of inhospitable prison bars, an overseas tourist who was scaling the magnificent mountain composed of one huge red rock, slipped to an untimely death on the rock surface far below. The rescue team that converged upon the ill-fated visitor's body through conventionally inaccessible scrub, discovered an infant's weather-worn matinee jacket lying within meters of the lifeless climber. The tiny jacket fit Lindy's exact description of the jacket baby Azaria was wearing at the time of her disappearance, but which she obviously was unable to produce for the court. Mrs. Chamberlain was released from prison *the same day,* and an immediate inquiry led to her long overdue acquittal. She was free at last.[5]

Not quite. Under the crushing injustice, Lindy had become a radically different personality. She was no longer the woman Michael had married. They struggled, they tried, but they finally parted ways. Ultimately, they divorced. Life and trust in the old environment would never ever be the same. The media had done a thorough job on echoing the libel and slander nationwide. With little incentive to probe into the final chapter, much of Australia to this very day still assumes she was guilty. As you may well imagine, by this time the media was far too busy with other important matters to waste much time on underlining their culpability, and managed to find even less time for repentance. Lindy, after a time, remarried and moved overseas to try to forget and rebuild her shattered life.[6]

That was two decades ago, and, for a certainty, this type of blatant media error has happened many times over since then. But this account was so tragic, the weird assumptions that were electronically transformed into truth so bizarre, and the media so blatantly culpable, it had to be retold here.

I'm sure you know of similar accounts—not as diabolic, perhaps, but heartbreak is heartbreak, humiliation is humiliation and libel is libel. Only God knows how many more innocents are anguishing in a miscarriage of justice from their trial by the media, while this self-elected, ultimate-authority-on-everything goes unassailable on its sinister romp with more unsubstantiated and unchecked lies and rumors of lies.

> *Acquitting the guilty and condemning the innocent—the* LORD *detests them both* (Proverbs 17:15).

Nor can we ignore the nations that suffer demise at the whim of fickle and biased journalism. As we discussed in an earlier chapter, the crushing territorial rape of the innocents in Serbia was also electronically justified in the dubious revenge agenda upon a sole adversary—their maverick president—by the mere pronouncement of two only "democratically elected" world leaders. Ironically, at the time of the catastrophic NATO bombing of Serbia, "undemocratic" Mr. Milosevic enjoyed a near unanimous support of his entire nation, whereas the "democratically" elected Bill Clinton's national popularity was at an all-time low.[7] Shouldn't this be telling us something?

Never mind. Ken Bacon, press spokesman for the Americans, and the ever sly British spokesman, Jamie O'Shea—with the charitable finesse of CNN and the BBC—never ceased to assure us that decimating Serbs from a goodly distance was a blessed event for humankind. We were soothed with the wise counsel that destroying Serbian ancient heritage and crippling the crucial infrastructure of a nation that had been clinging to a desperate hope to retain their national homelands from terrorist Kosovo insurgents was the righteous way to go. And the rest of the world barely blinked.

> *So justice is far from us, and righteousness does not reach us. We look for light, but all is darkness; for brightness, but we walk in deep shadows. Like the blind we grope along the wall, feeling our way like men without eyes....We look for justice, but find none; for deliverance, but it is far away* (Isaiah 59:9-11b).

We spoke earlier in our chapter on democracy of the tragic injustice toward the Christians and animists in the southern Sudan, the Islamic torching of churches in Indonesia and the unjust conquest by that same nation of the western half of ethnically diverse and predominately Christian West New Guinea. There have been a few scattered newspaper reports, but for the most part, the electronic media in these horrendous injustices is deafeningly silent—in contrast to their usual judgmental innuendoes—of who the perpetrators might be. It appears that challenging the Islamic governments of Sudan and Indonesia are just not worth cluttering their busy agenda.[8]

But the monumental tragedy of distressingly biased media reporting is upon the tiny nation of Israel, who after 53 years of her modern history, is still struggling for survival in the midst of a tidal wave of Islamic venom. Since 1948, a major spotlight of international attention has again focused on this minute sliver of a state as in no time since the reigns of King David and King Solomon some 3000 years ago. Unlike those glorious years of Israel's exultation, however, most of the international clamor these days concentrates on turning up the heat on her demise and—if her ever-loving neighbors have their way—the ultimate destruction of Israel as a nation.

Having spent the months of September and October 2000 in Jerusalem, when traveling on certain roads, even as visitors we had to keep an eye open for attacks by Palestinian terrorists using live ammunition. We encountered firsthand the highly organized and orchestrated uprising of the Palestinian Authority at the behest of Yasser not-so-noble Peace-Prize Arafat. But I was utterly aghast on returning home. The totally perverted media reports being fed to the Australian people were beyond belief. The interpretation by the journalists on the ground—if not aided and abetted by the local newsrooms—were an incomprehensible reversal of reality. The victims—in this case the Israelis—were actually the ones being accused of the crime via the media. As long recognized and rarely avoided, "The first casualty in any war is always truth."

Yet who even wants to take the time to entertain factual evidence when there is so much other violent confrontation, charges and counter charges around the globe? Moreover, "those people in the Middle East have been butchering each other for 4000 years, and this is hardly a priority on my program at the moment; let them blame whoever they like." Thus, when no one really cares, facts are hardly essentials on the agenda—unless Israel *does* happen to be on God's calendar at the moment. And unless the Bible is true after all:

> *This is what the* LORD *Almighty says: "In a little while I will once more shake the heavens and the earth, the sea and the dry land. I will shake all nations, and the desired of all nations will come, and I will fill this house with glory," says the* LORD *Almighty* (Haggai 2:6-7).

Fact is fact and truth is truth. But when we see reporters align themselves with but one conspicuous side of an issue, when they befriend themselves for whatever reason with their own choice of combatants, we must realize that we have a frightful, powerful, and unassailable voice upon the globe. It is a new mouthpiece that tramples truth in the mire, and speaks as a shiny new and universal god-voice to enlighten the planet. Truth is now manufactured instead of reported!

In his time, the less than reverent Pontius Pilate, presuming that there may even be such an item, cynically asked of Jesus, "What is truth?"[9] Our would-be deities today are one up on profane old Pontius. They mass produce the stuff themselves!

In those early days of the September 2000 Palestinian *intifada*, I had the less than joyful opportunity to surface in a small Jerusalem hotel, just across the hall from a few of the European photographers who earn their money from blood—obviously the more blood the more money. And there is also the inverse corollary of the principle: The smaller the victim, the greater the pay!

Remember Mohammed Dura, the 12-year-old Palestinian boy, whose picture in a pool of blood was flashed on television sets around the globe in the early days of the September 2000 Palestinian uprising? The propagation of that photo was engineered specifically to vilify Israel to the world via fabricated propaganda on the inhumanity of Israelis. Critical forensic research eventually proved conclusively that from the positions and angles of fire, the lad could not possibly have been hit by the Israelis. Moreover, film analysis revealed that the boy was shot from very close range, which could only have been by the Palestinian insurgents firing from immediately behind him.[10] But by the time the factual report came out, CNN was long gone. Needless to say, the French photographer clutching his hard earned pay-out, had cleared out even faster!

This diabolical voice is a new and unapproachable force on the planet. Our former God you could talk to—plead with.

There was forgiveness and there was understanding, even when you whispered. This new chief honcho is electronic and quite out of reach. It has no "sympathy sensors." Have you ever attempted to make your point with a recorded message? Have you tried arguing with an answering service? This is a breed of authority, a new overlord dominating humankind, a new deity for the Big Village, which, remember, was never even democratically elected!

Never mind, our original God of the Universe wasn't elected either! Possibly this is why there is such an intense battle currently being waged for final supremacy. Will the real God please stand up. Don't worry. He will!

1 See 1 Samuel 4:1-22.

2 "Public Opinion and the Media" by Paul Eidelberg, *Jerusalem Post,* January 5, 1992.

3 Ibid.

4 See Phil Ward, *Azaria* (Marion Rd, Netley, 5037, Australia: Griffin Press Ltd., 1984); John Bryson, *Evil Angels* (Sydney: Hodder Headline Australia, 1985).

5 A bizarre epilogue to Mrs. Chamberlin's release was a strongly worded advice to the court from the German pharmaceutical company which had manufactured the reagent used to identify fetal blood in the Chamberlin trial. The report reemphasized that the reagent used for blood testing was incorrect and in no way should the results have been used for a criminal investigation. Apparently an earlier similar statement issued during the trial at the request of the defense was discounted by the court. The long delayed repeat warning ironically arrived at the court office almost simultaneously to the discovery of the baby's jacket near the tourist's body, together resulting in the immediate release of Mrs. Chamberlain.

6 Ken Crispin, *Lindy Chamberlain: The Full Story* (Anguin, CA: Pacific Press Publishing Association, 1988); also Ken Crispin, *The Crown vs. Chamberlain* (Sydney: Albatross Books, 1987).

7 This is hardly to say that Mr. Milosevic or his officers committed no crimes, but it is to point out the utter disregard of justice in one-sided media accusations, avoiding mention of the terrorist activities of the so-called Kosovo Liberation Army, including their origins, purpose and agenda as well as omission of accurate reasons for NATO involvement. See also Chapter 2 "Democracy: Shall We Vote for Paul or Plato?"

8 For a report on worldwide persecution of Christians see "Year 2000 in Review," *The Voice of the Martyrs,* PO Box 443, Bartlesville, OK, December, 2000.

9 John 18:37-38.

10 "Palestinians, not Israelis, killed the 12-year-old boy," *Arutz 7 News,* October 31, 2000. For a damning visual indictment of those actually guilty see www.projectonesoul/Israel2/Israel2.htm

Trumpets So Loud We Can't Hear Them!

It's already been over a decade ago that I was flying in a small commuter aircraft in the short hop from Detroit to Cleveland in the USA. Cruising low over the once beckoning blue waters of Lake Erie, I was aghast. It had degenerated to a grungy green sewer. I remembered as a young boy the occasional anticipated family outings to Erie's pleasant beaches and enticing indigo blue waves. Not anymore! Rudyard Kipling's great gray-green greasy Limpopo River could not have been exemplified more graphically. Erie's innocent beauty had departed—her halo burned out.

My mind darted abruptly to the dramatically predicted scenario of Revelation 8:10, where the third angel blasted on his trumpet and "A third of the waters turned bitter." Like that unsolicited moment of truth, I cannot help but think of Jeremiah's woeful pronouncement and adapt it to our own present scenario: "The harvest is past, the summer is ended..." but why haven't we been hearing those angel trumpets?[1] Could it be that we have been too pre-programmed with faulty assumptions to even notice those shrill blasts, much less interpret them for what they are?

Today, Erie's locals, who once again take pride in their beloved beaches, like to point out that their more recent concentrated ecological efforts have well paid off in cleaning up the once polluted waters of their prestigious lake. But what about the rest of our deteriorating globe, from cracks in the myriad of crumbling worldwide "Chernobyls" to the phenomenal burn-off rate of Brazil and countless other Third World nations? What about the thousands of other locally polluted sites around the world whose good citizens have neither the finances, the infrastructures nor the capabilities to turn the clock back on their once pristine surroundings? I have seen much of this with my own eyes throughout the developing world. The disturbing and unnerving awakening remains: Stand back—a planet under demolition.

I suggest we take a hard look at those trumpets—shofars or ram's horns in Hebrew—of Revelation 8 and ponder the lengthening shadows of our day. The impassive may yawn and dismiss the warnings as yet another of "cry wolf"—one more chewing of a sensationalist cud. The unfazed ostriches among us, with sand yet on their eyelids, dream their own dreams of things to come. Some presume they won't still be around to participate. The clever of yet another brain wave, are certain that man always has and always will be able to resolve his own problems, and, by all means, they still have a day or so left to get on top of it. But the wise grip harsh reality in all its context and appropriate the Proverb:

> *Do not forsake wisdom, and she will protect you; love her, and she will watch over you* (Proverbs 4:6).

A spectacular seven angel pageant played out in the "trumpet chapters" of the Book of Revelation presents a chilling scenario for which most people would rather watch the science fiction movie than personally participate:

Then the angel took the censer, filled it with fire from the altar, and hurled it on the earth; and there came peals of thunder, rumblings, flashes of lightning and an earthquake (Revelation 8:5).

Speaking of earthquakes, there have been a few hefty ones hit in various places lately and a few more big ones presumed not to be too far around the corner. But not to get sidetracked and miss the core essence of our celestial drama, let's keep an eye on what these angels are about to do:

The first angel sounded his trumpet, and there came hail and fire mixed with blood, and it was hurled down upon the earth (Revelation 8:7a).

Before we proceed any further, I have a question: Do you suppose by any stretch of the imagination, the Almighty might choose to encode cosmic hail from heaven as filthy old SCUD missiles?

One should be aware that "heaven" in both Hebrew and Greek is quite simply termed as "sky." Of course, this is frequently differentiated as sometimes two, sometimes three or even up to seven levels of "the heavens," depending on which rabbi you may happen to be chatting with. In much Hebrew cosmology, the first domain is where birds fly. Above that might be the elevation of the cloud patterns, and the highest heaven of all—be it the third, fifth or seventh layer depending on who's counting—is the domain of the Almighty. Included as well would be a vast invisible spiritual realm, referred to in the Scriptures as "the Host of Heaven," not all of which are exclusively the "good guys," I should point out. Latest scrutiny by the Hubble Space Telescope has not yet reported any observed mile markers out there at this point in time. So with the absence of any specific celestial signposts, heaven is part of the sky, and some of the sky—but not all—may well be heaven.[2] The terminology, like the real thing, is a bit nebulous!

Whether we like him or not, Saddam's SCUDs technically did "fall from heaven." When Mr. Clinton's cruise missiles descended upon and scorched the earth of Serbia in like fashion, they utilized the same route. Or should any future megalomaniac choose to release his lethal venom, in the near or not so near future, his rocketry will surge forward through quite the same air space. The "heavens" can and will be temporarily borrowed for purposes of mass incineration by terrorists, tyrants or totalitarian regimes of all stripes, whether they be "democratically elected" or egocentrically selected. Make no mistake. We have been forewarned. The aftereffects follow:

A third of the earth was burned up, a third of the trees were burned up, and all the green grass was burned up (Revelation 8:7b).

I will be quick to point out that the angel's censer of cause-and-effect contained more than one item of divinely permitted retribution. There were three: "Hail and fire mixed with blood." That is, we hardly have to wait for more SCUD or cruise missiles alone to properly evaluate what all of humankind has—by our own depravity—duly invited upon our own heads. Let's look at additional tragic turf where an already partially incinerated world can even now acknowledge, "Been there, done that":

How many in the Western World took seriously, or even understood, the global devastation wrought by the El Niño effects in 1998? Smoke haze over the sprawling Asian giant of

Indonesia contributed to at least one major maritime disaster and one airline catastrophe, but that was piddling compared to the defoliation and the havoc wreaked upon the gardens, grass, trees, and the ecological plight of the fourth most populous nation on earth. Moreover, this burning, smoldering and parched desolation spread right across the vast island nation of Papua New Guinea, the second largest island in the world, and peopled by some 800 individual languages or "mini-nations," as it were. From there, this calamitous drought, unprecedented in recent geological records, spread right throughout the entire Pacific Island nations and into the western reaches of Latin America.

The United States and the rest of the world were ultimately affected as well with the inverse repercussions—a final playing out of the original climatic disturbances with massive downpours, flooding and fierce tornadoes in the opposite hemisphere. Was it a mini-preview of God's wrath? Or was it even more likely a furious atmospheric rebuttal to mankind's indifference to the responsibility of caring for the priceless land resources that God has given him? Or was it both?

So then, what can we make of this prophecy—a foretaste or otherwise—of the latter half of verse 7 above? Those of us who lived through that unprecedented drought in regions that normally exceed 10 feet of rainfall a year, may be inclined to take it more seriously than others.

These meteorological reprimands do give us yet a second representation of the distress and anguish foretold in verse 7 and reflect an admonition quite apart from those other manmade afflictions of SCUD or cruise missiles-cum-fiery hail in the first part of the verse. And have you noticed that the Ancient of Days does not even seem to be the one pulling the trigger!

And, finally, there's one other man-made debacle of ominous dimensions that we must yet ponder. As a young nuclear scientist in the 1950s, I worked for a number of years at the plutonium manufacturing facility at Hanford, Washington, in the USA. Our specific laboratory monitored the surrounding environment to maintain an adequate level of safety standards from any and all of the harmful radioactive wastes and effluents.

Routine emissions were carefully monitored, and the daily levels that were recorded were judged to be safe enough for the environment in those days. But "those days" are not "these days," and now 50 years on, unthinkable pollution problems are surfacing from the early engineering and long-term storage of the lethal nuclear materials, some of which will remain highly radioactive for thousands of years.

In a feature article in the *Oregonian* in July 1992, which documented the ongoing environmental degeneration spanning over 50 years of plutonium production, it was reported that at least 66 of the 178 massive underground concrete storage tanks were cracked, leaking and noxiously seeping into an immense area of the underground water table. By that point in time, the gigantic underground plume of deadly radioactive contamination had bulged over an area of some 200 square miles within the Columbia River Basin to a depth of up to 200 feet. Obviously, this has only degenerated further in the last decade of ever-broadening and irreversible pollution.[3]

This nuclear nightmare is one more tragic picking from that ever-so-enticing fruit on a now modernized "tree of knowledge of good and evil" that once touched, will never go away.[4] And quite as unwelcome as the odious waste—so much more so, the horrific weapon. At this point in time, nuclear advantage is intensely being sought by Iraq and Iran along with a few other outsiders to the coveted nuclear club. Most chillingly, multimillionaire Osama bin Laden, arch-potentate of all terrorists, is reported to now own at least three of his prized nuclear trophies—presumably bargained off by a few hard-up Soviet generals—tucked away somewhere in Afghanistan for his long-awaited day in the sun.

Unfortunately, Hanford is but one pinhead of all the nuclear facilities now dotted across the planet. One of the larger pinheads, it is true, but nevertheless only one of a mixed bag of the ever-mushrooming potential points of disaster.

In 1967 at a similar installation at Chelyabinsk, a former Soviet weapons facility in the Ural Mountains, there was an underground tank or even tanks which spontaneously created a violent explosion monitored in the west. In those days, no information whatsoever leaked from the highly secretive Soviet pressure cooker, so no one knows—or ever will know—the scope of that disaster, including how many people actually died. Some USA scientists fear that a devastation of even greater magnitude will ultimately happen at Hanford as well.[5]

The Three Mile Island incident, in a reasonably urban area near Philadelphia in 1979, was but peanuts compared to the larger lethal emissions, which both have occurred and will certainly continue to occur with even greater irreversible noxious degradation. Most of these incidents—if, indeed, reported—have been the first warning bells that all is not well on the planet the Eternal One has loaned to us. The moment of truth is that in this countless proliferation of nuclear sites around the globe, the structural soundness of all those earlier on "cold war" facilities—along with their then known precautions and safety standards—have long passed their use-by dates. Indeed, the god of progress has well peppered our planet with radioactive seeds from the tree of knowledge. Or is the preferred word salt instead of pepper? Jesus once said, "Everyone will be salted with fire."[6] Whatever the Son of Man might actually have meant by that, our guess could perhaps be getting a bit warm, if we pause to reflect for a moment upon this vast global expansion of aging and crumbling nuclear reactors.

Of course, the classic pilot run to domestic disaster was the cataclysmic Chernobyl debacle of April 26, 1986. It was a full 10 days before the Soviet authorities finally made a brief announcement to their people—including those in the area of closest proximity to Chernobyl—that a "slight irregularity" had occurred at the nuclear reactor. That was all—an irregularity! Meanwhile the local populace in the immediate vicinity were dying like flies. I have a personal friend from that general region in the Ukraine whose sister's arms suddenly turned white and scaly from unwittingly washing her family's clothes in contaminated water. No one was told anything! Nor did anyone know of the man-made angel of death who had silently crept into their community.

At the time of this writing, Chernobyl has just marked the 15th commemoration of its infamous demise. Thus far 30,000 people are known to have perished directly from this catastrophe of human culpability. To add to that dreaded day of remembrance, it was almost simultaneously announced by more than troubled engineers, that serious new cracks were progressively widening in the massive sarcophagus-like concrete tomb of the ill-fated reactor. They fear for its ultimate total collapse. And should that ever happen, Chernobyl II would be no less devastating throughout the Ukraine, across Russia and into the rest of Europe than was the horrific Chernobyl I.

Perhaps it's time to follow up on that first angel of Revelation 8:7 with a bit more Scripture:

The second angel sounded his trumpet, and something like a huge mountain, all ablaze, was thrown into the sea. A

third of the sea turned into blood, a third of the living crea-
tures in the sea died, and a third of the ships were de-
stroyed. The third angel sounded his trumpet, and a great
star, blazing like a torch, fell from the sky on a third of the
rivers and on the springs of water—the name of the star is
Wormwood*. A third of the waters turned bitter, and many*
people died from the waters that had become bitter
(Revelation 8:8-11, emphasis mine).

Remarkably, the precise meaning of the word *chernobyl* in
the Ukrainian language is a worthless, contemptible black
reed-like plant that abounds in the area. And it is this very
word, *chernobyl*, that was used in the more than a century old
version of the Ukrainian Bible to translate the name for that
blazing star in Revelation 8:11. Moreover, the word used in
the neighboring Russian Bible is again the name of a closely
related and likewise bitter plant, but which has an added feature of a hollow stem of evident fragility. The original term
both from Hebrew, Greek and, finally, English is "wormwood"—bitter—an absolutely bitter, contemptible plant.

In Bible translation in a country which does not have exactly the same flora and fauna of the original language, one
translates the word into the nearest natural equivalent of the
target language. The translator searches not necessarily for an
equivalent plant or animal that looks like the original, but
which does the same things. In the Ukrainian translation, the
bitter chernobyl plant was chosen, and in Russian the *polyñ*
plant was selected to represent the bitter wormwood from the
original Hebrew.

Does it make you wonder who tipped off those translators,
over a century ago with insight on which words to use to
match up with the eventual Chernobyl disaster of 1986?

Worthless, contemptible, bitter, hollow, empty and bitter again—I also wonder what in the world we were doing that we didn't hear that trumpet in 1986 when the blazing star Wormwood-cum-Chernobyl took front and center stage? Perhaps some of us did! You know who else did? When that dire catastrophe devastated the Ukraine, all those citizens who knew a bit about the Bible—and a fair number did—recognized immediately the corresponding significance of that third angel of Revelation 8:11. But, unfortunately, CNN must have forgotten to tell the rest of us at the time!

Is the point getting through that these so-presumed "mad prophet" predictions of two millennia ago have already surfaced in ample preview in our own backyards, while just as in Noah's day, "marrying and giving in marriage," "buying and selling," and all manner of fun and games continues unabated. We have been marvelously conditioned not to blink—or is it think? Of course, the probability that any one of these hiccups to the norm may happen every so often throughout history is a given. But for the scenario of all seven of the trumpets to ominously raise their nasty notes within the space of a few short decades—if not years—is a major flashing red light on the control panel of time and space.

We all know that dogs can hear vibrations that we humans can't pick up. So it must be with those celestial shofars. Some will hear them a bit better than others. This is hardly new. Remember when Jesus taught in parables, and even those disciples on the inside track got a bit hung up? He would then have to march them into a corner and say, "Look, not everyone is going to get this, but you guys have been around long enough to be picking it up. That's why I use parables. Some out there will just not come in on my wave length."[7]

So it is with trumpets, *shofars*, that is. There are quite a few out there who just won't be able to pick up the pitch with ordinary ears. But for the rest: He who has ears to hear, let him hear (Luke 14:35).[8]

Probably it is time we evaluate the essence of these "one-third" measurements, but first let's take a look at the fourth angel trumpet in the series:

> *The fourth angel sounded his trumpet, and a third of the sun was struck, a third of the moon, and a third of the stars, so that a third of them turned dark. A third of the day was without light, and also a third of the night* (Revelation 8:12).

In the account of our fourth angel blasting his trumpet warning, the celestial bodies are going to be dimmed a tad and the days are going to be a bit dark and the nights even darker. Sounds like it might get a shade smoky perhaps. And with Iran all lined up to crash the nuclear club, and Saddam Hussein right behind them, this blast—trumpet or otherwise—could be sooner rather than later. (I didn't mention this earlier on, but some reports say Saddam already does have the necessary bits and pieces for a nuclear device now.) Both of these nations are in a neck-and-neck race to see which one gets the kudos for "teaching Israel a lesson." Anyway, our lesson is that it will probably get a bit darker before the Light appears.

We need to reflect on the significance of these "one-third" measurements. With the first angel, a third of the vegetation is destroyed. With the second, a third of the living creatures perish in the sea. That sounds like another pretty mean case of marine pollution, and brings to mind the seemingly routine occurrences of nasty oil spills from both before and after the infamous Exxon Valdez spill in Alaska in March 1989.[9]

The ugliest one in history was when 240 million gallons of crude oil oozed into the Persian Gulf off Kuwait and Saudi Arabia in 1991. The next nearest to that yucky level was into the Gulf of Mexico in 1980, with others in the Shetland Islands, the Azores, off the coastline of Greece, into the North Sea, another off Genoa, and the one in Sydney Harbor. Oil pollution into the sea is becoming so commonplace these days that many spills no longer even make the front pages. The news fades. But the long-term degradation of the environment lingers on.

Our third angel precedes the dread Chernobyl phenomenon, and the prediction of a horrendous poisoning of a third of the earth's fresh water sources. So who dares to forget the cynical encore to the so-renamed "northern Chernobyl" with the incomprehensible devastation wrought on January 30, 2000, by the mammoth cyanide spill into the Lepos and Samos Rivers in Romania, on into the "crown jewel" Tisza River of Hungary, and finally into the legendary Danube of Hungary, Serbia and Bulgaria. When a dam serving a gold mining venture in Romania ruptured, 100,000 cubic meters of deadly polluted waters of 200 times the permissible level of deathly cyanide surged into Central Europe's river systems, poisoning the entire food chain of fish, birds and all manner of aquatic flora.[10]

Hungary dubbed the catastrophe their Aquatic Chernobyl! They tried to clean it all up. Several hundred tons of dead fish were scooped from the Tisza alone, and even that was deemed to be but the tip of the iceberg. Today, most of the rest of the world has forgotten. Life goes on. But may I ask where all that cyanide went, which passed the Danube delta into the sea? Water evaporates, but deathly chemicals in the food chain do not![11]

So to follow through with our "one-third" sequence, destruction of one-third of the vegetation of the earth, pollution of one-third of the earth's oceans and contamination of one-third of the planet's drinking water is a fairly large decimation, yet it is within comprehension. But the loss of "a third of the day" and a "third of the night," a "third of the sun" and a "third of the moon," seems a bit more cryptic. Perhaps we are only being told that we're going to see a lot more smoke than we have up to now.

There is another factor we should consider which brings this ratio of destruction much more into the reality of comprehending these other dire events we have already seen to be surfacing around us. One-third in a non-technical society—in the ancient Hebrew society—did not quite mean 33%. What it does mean is a significant enough dose to awaken the world—not that the entire world will wake up—but in a degree able to touch a pre-designated proportion of those involved. This type of estimated measurement—less than half, but a whopping big event—is commonplace in the non-technical societies of the Third World to this day. Again, I must note: "Been there, observed that."

Yet one more consideration—perhaps many folks quite unwittingly assume these dreadful deeds introduced by those first four angels will be taking shape right down the street somewhere. (And they certainly don't want to be there when it happens!)

Well, on one hand, many of them have already happened close at hand to multitudes of the unprepared, sometime somewhere, and will do so again. As we have already seen, the Most High has done a few test runs over the last decade or so to inform a skeptical planet that He has the wherewithal to accurately program exactly what He said He would do.

Moreover, His pilot projects indicate that His divine countdown is up and running and that all He has to do now is to let those determined to destroy themselves to go right ahead. He certainly does want to get our attention.

But on the other hand, many of us who share these pages might just have a slightly over-focused view only upon ourselves, presuming that all those fireworks might have been planned just for us. That's okay. We can all be prepared. With a third of the globe being somewhat involved (even by Hebraic standards), there could be a possible problem most anywhere, including our own backyards.

But the whole underlying truth is that the grand finale is not primarily programmed for Paris, London, New York or anywhere on Main Street, USA. We will find that the Scriptures give us only three major "I'll-be-sure-to-look-you-up" addresses for the final countdown in humanity's ultimate challenge to divine authority. A more than compensating—if not comforting—feature to those awesome announcements by the seven angels is the concluding and triumphant promise of the Everlasting One:

> *Now the dwelling of God is with men, and he will live with them. They will be his people, and God himself will be with them and be their God. He will wipe every tear from their eyes. There will be no more death or mourning or crying or pain, for the old order of things has passed away* (Revelation 21:3-4).

But where might this all take place? Of the top three priority venues we pointed to above, the first and foremost is a reestablished and renewed Jerusalem:

> *In the last days the mountain of the LORD's temple will be*

established as chief among the mountains; it will be raised above the hills, and all nations will stream to it. Many peoples will come and say, "Come let us go up to the mountain of the LORD, to the house of the God of Jacob. He will teach us his ways, so that we may walk in his paths." The law will go out from Zion, the word of the LORD from Jerusalem. He will judge between the nations and will settle disputes for many peoples. They will beat their swords into plowshares and their spears into pruning hooks. Nation will not take up sword against nation, nor will they train for war anymore (Isaiah 2:2-4).

The second is Damascus:

See, Damascus will no longer be a city but will become a heap of ruins (Isaiah 17:1b).

And the third is Babylon:

Babylon, the jewel of kingdoms, the glory of the Babylonians' pride, will be overthrown by God like Sodom and Gomorrah (Isaiah 13:19).

And one more for Babylon:

Babylon has fallen, has fallen! All the images of its gods lie shattered on the ground! (Isaiah 21:9b).[12]

Certainly there are other lands and cities throughout the Scriptures that have a prophetic focus for both better or worse in the end of days. Nor should anyone think that the last days events in these three cities will not also substantially impact— both literally and symbolically—upon the entire globe.

Those who do not know their Bibles, and those who *think they know* the Scriptures but fail to appropriate the divine thread of destiny that is woven from the Garden of Eden to the soon-to-come City of God, may ignorantly charge that I have selectively picked on Damascus and Babylon (and her associations) out of a haystack of other texts. Not so. This entire concept reflecting the idolatrous versus the divine is constant throughout the Scriptures, and is the sum and substance of the final test match between the Most High and the "rest of the world."

Most significantly, these two biblically disreputable cities, represent not one but two antichrists[13] —the final two challengers to the King of the Universe at the end of days. One represents a relentless supremacy challenge to the God of Israel. This "religious" type rivalry once flourished in the days of the Kings of Israel and Judah. It resurfaced in the 7th century AD via the teachings of Mohammed and has now gained hurricane fury in our day. Damascus always has been and always will be the flagship of pagan forces that impudently vied with the living God. But Damascus never yet has been destroyed to become a "heap of ruins." If the Bible is, indeed, true, it ultimately will be.

The other city is representative of an apostate, idolatrous and humanistic Jezebel-styled alternative to any and all claims and standards to the character and purpose of the God of the Bible. Symbolic Jezebel is featured in infamous fashion throughout the Book of Revelation. While Damascus is the far more bloody of the pair of challengers, Babylon is the far more subtle and, therefore, far more dangerous.

Physical Babylon, by contrast has long been overthrown, but symbolically her deadly wound has been healed—for now. She no longer symbolizes a primitive paganism, but a sophisticated and despicably idolatrous global force vying for supremacy against the Ancient of Days.

And finally Jerusalem, like her coming King, will be what she will be. These three entities are the focal point of the final action in days to come, and that most probably, not too far down the track.

This is the very reason so many Bible believers are awakening in these days to keep their eyes on Jerusalem and what God Almighty promised to do to renovate and restore this city and this nation. Please recognize it. This is Bible prediction from Genesis to Revelation. The present attraction of a mushrooming number of the faithful to this land is far afield from a sentimental tour to see the ancient biblical sites of days gone by. It is rather a preview visit "home" for the weary and waiting to observe firsthand those divine pieces of the promises that are already beginning to fall into place for His big day—the Day of the Lord.

The amazement to me is why so many other Christians are failing to sense what is now going on under our very noses. That is, what do they read in their Bibles? Or perhaps they are not reading them at all!

I would be very cautious about trying to tell you what is going to happen and when. We have already seen too many foolish failures in our day. But I have no problems telling you what is now happening according to the prophets—namely our first four *shofar* blasting angels and the present reality of their predictions. These are now; these are for real; and they are ongoing.

But there is certainly one future event and venue of which I am totally convinced—World War III is only a matter of time in the Middle East. As I write these pages, Arafat's intifada is nearing a boil. His cohorts in Iraq, Iran and Syria are aligning their agendas for strategy. Saddam in particular is rubbing his hands together spoiling for a showdown as I write. These are truly days of destiny!

When will be the flash point? Who knows? How long will it take? Israel's wars usually don't last long. It could be over in 3-1/2 days—or this one could take as long as 3-1/2 years; or somewhere in between. That's irrelevant. It's not our business. The Almighty provided us with Bibles, not calendars! Our business is to:

- Know our Bible
- Establish our priorities
- Know our God.

1   See Jeremiah 8:20.

2   Reference *The New Bible Dictionary* (London: Inter-Varsity Press, 1962).

3   "Hanford: Consequences will last thousands of years," *The Sunday Oregonian,* July 18, 1992.

4   Genesis 2:15-17; 3:1-19.

5   "Tanks at Hanford Could Explode," *The Sunday Oregonian,* July 18, 1992.

6   Mark 9:49.

7   Matthew 13:13-15 and Mark 4:11-12.

8   In addition to Luke 14:35, this text has 14 additional occurrences, the most often repeated command in the New Testament.

9   The Exxon Valdez spill, as devastating as it was, was even small in comparison to ongoing spillage around the world. It received much more attention, however, because it occurred in the United States, as well as the enormous settlement paid out by the oil company.

10 Gusztáv Kosztolányi's Csardas, *Aquatic Chernobyl Requiem for the Tisza and the Szamos: Parts I-IV;* http://www.ce-review.org/00/7/csardas7.html

11 Ibid.

12 Compare also with a wider symbolic reference to Babylon in Revelation 17:5 and Revelation 18:1-24.

13 Compare the plural with 1 John 2:18b.

CHAPTER 6

The Pit and the Pandemonium

We still have a few more angels—complete with *shofars*—to observe.

We can summarize those first four in the previous chapter to be intriguingly associated with ecological disasters, salt-water as well as fresh water pollution, destruction of the ozone layer, flood and drought in the wake of catastrophic climate changes, vast global areas of burn-off and the corresponding atmospheric pollution.

That does sound familiar, does it not, or don't you monitor the daily world news? Pretty lucky, that future-forecasting John fellow, to come up with that kind of meteorological and ecological accuracy—not to mention the SCUD missiles—from so long ago. I'm sure you know by now that there is no such thing as "luck," but only the Grand Planner who Himself is quite a stickler for precision.

Anyway, we received our introduction to global warming and climate change—and much, much more—from our four angel friends with *shofars*, for which much of humanity unfortunately has little ear. Nevertheless, we, who hope to have an ear to hear, have three more angels to go to round out the complete seven.

And the pageant surrounding angel number five goes like this:

*The fifth angel sounded his trumpet, and I saw a star that had fallen from the sky to the earth. The star was given the key to the shaft of the Abyss. When he opened the Abyss, smoke rose from it like the smoke from a gigantic furnace. The sun and sky were darkened by the smoke from the Abyss. And out of the smoke locusts came down upon the earth and were given power like that of scorpions of the earth. They were told not to harm the grass of the earth or any plant or tree, but **only those people who did not have the seal of God** on their foreheads* (Revelation 9:1-4, emphasis mine).*

Now that is unquestionably awesome, and makes me inexpressibly grateful that I—as an otherwise helpless human entity—have been filled and sealed with the Spirit of the Living God. This is the same God who in the beginning hovered over the darkened waters and initially breathed life into a faceless universe—and who has Himself sealed me with an ample measure of divine covering for any and all difficult days to come.[1] However, it is not this glorious gleam of hope—as encouraging as that might be—that is our primary focus in our text at hand, which reflects the somber scenario following *shofar* number five.

What we really must note is what it is in the smoke that comes churning out of that perilous pit? What is the analogy—if not reality—of the locusts that deliver pain like scorpions? We need no science fiction here, please, to mesmerize the mind! This is for real. We are herewith forewarned of an unprecedented scourge of down-to-earth demons that have been given release to plague the planet.

No demons around here, do I hear someone say? Let me mention a few incidents to refresh your memory. April 20,

1999. Columbine High School, Littleton, Colorado, USA. Nothing suspicious there! Didn't notice any weird looking creatures with horns and pitchforks. Only automatic weapons, 12 murdered students and one teacher and blood all over the place!

Nor dare we forget all the other demonically inspired mass murders—school-oriented and otherwise—before and after Columbine. On November 5, 1999, a Texas schoolboy wrote a class essay—fortunately it turned out to be fiction—on his plans to murder his teacher and classmates. Just another routine school day! In that same infamous week, a crazed gunman in a Seattle shipyard kills four, a medical student in Brazil attacks a film audience with a machine gun and leaves two dead and four wounded, and a technician in Hawaii murders seven in a blaze of self-styled glory. Yet these once unthinkable blood-lettings are becoming so commonplace with multiple copy-cat occurrences around the world, it no longer warrants prime media attention.

Here's another scenario. Have you ever involved yourself in the hellish inner-city drug and alcohol scenes, complete with gang wars, prostitution, rapes and sex slavery? There is no future, there is no hope, there is no help in sight for hundreds of millions trapped in the sewers of forsaken humanity and the swarming urban pits of hell. Nothing suspicious there either, I would suppose! Is it any wonder that youth suicide is the leading cause of death for under 30-year-olds in Australia, as well as reaching epidemic proportions throughout most other regions of the western world?[2]

Or have you shuddered at the worldwide scourge of pedophilia and child pornography that has diabolically infested the Internet, not to mention the pornographic plague in general that is endemically defiling all levels of society? What happens to all those missing kids? Thousands from the gutters of the Third World do not even have a shelter to call home. These destitute children, cursed and discarded by a depraved society, like insects to be trodden underfoot are never even missed. Are any of those who have disappeared from within the developed world and who are searched for ever located? Alive? Still no demonic forces at work in this day and time, is it yet presumed?

We hardly dare suggest that good people have not tried to help. Even the politicians have raised the occasional cry for compassion. But, unfortunately, in almost all civil efforts, the Almighty has been set aside on a redundancy package, and more politically correct techniques have been applied, particularly in the realm of linguistic adjustment. To reduce the pain and stigma of prostitution, it is now re-labeled the "sex industry," while addiction is eased to an illness, which sadly without consulting our Maker, is seldom cured. Outright rejection of help from an Abba who cares is standard mentality, while the demonic tentacles grasp more and more firmly into a global society which has jettisoned the only God than can and will help.

There are even other far more fiendish forces afoot. With all the resolutions and the platitudes of the United Nations, alongside the well-meaning—but frequently not too brilliant—efforts of all the placard waving, peace promoting groups, all the amnesty (read: amnesty for a preferred agenda) and care groups, not even a dent is made in the epidemic-like escalation of worldwide massacres and bloodshed.

A report crossing my desk only last night projected that the death toll including massacre, starvation, disease and deprivation in the 32 months of the Congolese war to April 2001 is now approaching 3 million, which tops the formerly incomprehensible 2 million who were annihilated in the bloody 1960s in Sudan.[3]

Who among us can even comprehend the enormity of this inhumanity? These are real people; God-created and God-loved neighbors on the planet. It is reported as well that some hundreds of thousands were butchered in the Hutu-Tutsi massacres in Rwanda and Burundi nearly a decade ago. The rebels and counter rebels in Uganda, the Democratic Republic of the Congo and Sierra Leone, are to name only a few more of the conflicts of more indelible memory. To these we can add the ethnically embittered government of Zimbabwe and the ongoing "ethnic cleansing" of the Christian south by the present Islamic government of Sudan to add to the river of blood that incessantly flows across Africa.

Oh, yes, did I hear someone out there concede that, well, there could perhaps yet be a few demons still playing up in places like Africa?

Then there have been horrendous massacres in the Balkans from three contenders—not only Serbs as the media has often been so prone to reflect! Islamic fundamentalists have murdered several hundred thousand of their more moderate countrymen since Algerian independence from France in 1962. As already noted in an earlier chapter, Hafez al Assad, the despot of Syria, annihilated 20,000 of his countrymen in 1982 to maintain a grip on his totalitarian authority,[4] while Saddam Hussein gassed 5000 Kurds to their deaths to force the lid of his own evil regime down upon his enemies.[5] Much more recently the Islamic riots in Indonesia have butchered thousands of Christians throughout the island archipelago including massacres of the non-Malay Melanesians of West Papua.[6]

Fewer perhaps in overall death rate but no less depraved in

design, inner city villains periodically brutally bash—and some-times murder—the aged and helpless, robbing them of their meager pensioner pennies to support their diabolically driven need of a fix. And these once unthinkable, contemptible crimes are recurring with greater and greater frequency.

No demonic plague? Let me assure you that the cover of that pit has been well and truly ajar for many days on end, and is ever widening its sinister breach. Our world is by now well engulfed within a global scourge of unassailable evil that is spi-raling out of control as time slips by.

We had been tipped off in advance. We should have known!

> *Therefore rejoice, you heavens and you who dwell in them! But woe to the earth and the sea, because the devil has gone down to you! He is filled with fury, because he knows that his time is short* (Revelation 12:12).

Yet there are those who say, "But I didn't plan on still being around here for that kind of a grim scene." You know what? That's what I was also led to believe when I was a young fellow. It sounded okay, and it didn't seem to me that there's too much wrong with being out of town when the storm clouds roll in. But as I got older and started getting serious with the Scriptures, I found out that the God of the storm was, in fact, giving me a sanctified umbrella and telling me to get out there and help those poor folks who didn't have one.

Actually, I became awakened not a little when I translated the Scriptures—the book of Revelation, in fact—for the Waola Tribe in the highlands of Papua New Guinea back in the 1960's and 1970's. I gradually realized then that some of the pieces of what I had assumed to be true about the end times just couldn't be made to fit together. And then I understood that what I had been told was far more theory—if not wistful thinking—than it was Bible. But we're not going to get into that now. That's another bit of insight for another chapter down the line. The reality is that that evil pit of abomination is already wide open, and *we are still here!*

Moreover, our moment of truth is buttressed by the fact that Messiah has not yet made His much promised redemptive appearance for crunch time. But, shall I encourage you, we are getting ever closer. Anyone sealed with the Spirit of the Almighty may breathe much more easily than those less unfortunate ones who know nothing of the divine provision of His protective anointing.

I want to point out that I am suggesting nothing spooky whatsoever at this divine seal bit. It is as basic as whispering, "Please, Lord"—but meaning it! It is nothing more—and certainly nothing less—than the kind of relationship your Abba in heaven had intended to hold with you from before you were born. How does this sound:

> He *will cover you with his feathers, and under his wings will you find refuge; his faithfulness will be your shield and rampart. You will not fear the terror of night, nor the arrow that flies by day, nor the pestilence that stalks in the darkness, nor the plague that destroys at midday. A thousand may fall at your side, ten thousand at your right hand, but it will not come near you* (Psalm 91:4-7).

In a final wrap-up of that ominous presentation of the fifth angel, John the Apostle, a prophetic spokesman of the Eternal One, told us precisely the evils that were to flood the earth in these days. Biblical preparation always has been and always will be on *how to stand,* not where to look for the nearest exit. The vision of the pit of evil that John saw must be recognized as a current reality to any and all who possess even a smidgen of honesty. But those who have honed a relationship with the Most High have little to fear. He is as good as His promise, and a divine umbrella is ready and waiting for all who claim its covering.

Therefore, let us move on to angel number six and one more *shofar* blast.

> *The sixth angel sounded his trumpet, and I heard a voice coming from the horns of the golden altar that is before God. It said to the sixth angel who had the trumpet, "Release the four angels who are bound at the great river Euphrates." And the four angels who had been kept ready for this very hour and day and month and year were released to kill a third of mankind. The number of the mounted troops was two hundred million. I heard their number* (Revelation 9:13-16).

I touched briefly on this prophetic scenario in a related context in an earlier book, *Where is the Body?* which may be of additional interest.[7] At this point we want to concentrate our focus specifically on that awesome militia of 200 million, its origins and where it may be headed. That is quite a few troops once you give it some pause for reflection.

Let us note that this happening appears to be rooted along the Euphrates River in the general turf of Saddam Hussein. However, we dare not lose sight of the fact that this may or may not be more symbolic than pinpoint. This SCUD-breathing anti-Semite does have an impressive range of contingent of kindred spirits in his part of the world, and particularly so when it comes to loathing Israel.

In the very month of this writing, terrorist-cum-statesman Arafat has been warming up to the dubious dictator with a bit of advance cash for the purchase of a "home away from home" somewhere in Iraq. A mutual darkroom deal or two as well, leaves us with Saddam, in turn, blossoming out in support of the arch terrorist's intensifying bloody *intifada* against Israel.[8] The Iraqi dictator is reported to have proposed to generously increase the Palestinians' "martyr" award of $2000 offered to the families of each young rioter sacrificed in the holy *jihad*.[9] But that was hardly all. This "peace loving" monarch of SCUD missiles has also graciously come up with the added injection of two million Iraqi volunteers complete with armor to be shortly stationed at the Jordanian and Syrian borders for the liberation of "Palestine" from the wicked "Zionist entity"![10]

So this pair of Israel haters are pretty much bosom buddies already. Moreover Saddam's ongoing lets-kiss-and-make-up initiatives throughout the pan-Arab region seem to have been paying off of late, and the dictator's patrons are visibly on the increase. Moreover, should he be their man to rid the Middle East of the wretched Zionists, they not only will forgive him for all the past, but give him all the oil he can drink! Thus the cited Euphrates River in our above Scripture text may figuratively stretch out a shade longer than Baghdad city center. And this is very significant.

However, the present two million Iraqi volunteers are not exactly two hundred million as you may have already noticed. The extremely interesting facet, therefore, is not this puny two-million-man regiment on hand at the moment, but the yet-to-surface super scout troop of 200 million! Now when I was younger, again I was informed with astute authority that a militia of this size could only emerge out of China. No other nation could begin to field such a massive number of troops.

Five decades down the track proves the paperback prophets wrong again. India today is an additional conceivable alternative, having entered into the ominous—to feed, at least—one billion club earlier this year. But the present reality, on either political or military grounds, give the nod to neither India nor China! Where is this army supposed to be headed, anyway?

Quite overlooked in the considerations of yesteryear has been the massive Muslim entity that today numbers 1.2 billion adherents and which ironically happens to be nearly identical to the population of today's China. Sprawling from the Islamic giant of Indonesia, on the Pacific Rim in the Far East, spanning most of Asia, stretching across the entire Arabic Middle East and finally across Islamic North Africa, all the way to the Muslim nations of Morocco and Mauritania, which bulge out into the Atlantic Ocean at its western extremity, this monstrous Islamic empire encompasses over 10,000 miles of the earth's surface. So should this be the source of the largest troop movement this planet has ever seen, pray tell where do you suppose this mega-militia might have a mind to go?

Should you have any lingering doubts, you might consult the Hebrew prophets, Zechariah, Joel and Isaiah or even Jesus Himself.[11] Jerusalem is the Holy Grail of Islamic appetite. Yet that may not even be the most perfect analogy. Islam does have Mecca and Medina for their holiest shrines, and for 1300 years Jerusalem was little more than a third-rate afterthought. That is, until the Jews came home to stay! In the Islamic sense of supremacy, hatred unequivocally must and does hold precedence over any other positive aspirations. So shall we re-identify it as the Jihad Grail of Jerusalem. There are no other options!

But let's focus on reality. It would not take 200 million volunteers to clean house with the 5 million Jews in miniature Israel. Certainly that patent howl for Israeli blood is the catch-cry of the Middle East at this very hour. But the might of the awesome Israeli Defense Force notwithstanding, a half dozen armies, air forces and an ample peppering of SCUD missiles with non-conventional warheads should surely gratify the aspirations of the much heralded Islamic *jihad*. This is currently the foremost cry in the local media throughout the Islamic Middle East, and it has been at the top of the "wish list" for most Arabic nations plus Iran for decades. So there are hardly any surprises, except for one. That is the embedded in concrete fact that none of the Western leaders have ever seemed to have quite grasped the point!

There's one more monumental detail to consider. Should any desecration large or small ever be committed against either or both of the two Muslim mosques proudly perched atop the ruins of Israel's two ancient temples on the Temple Mount, Islamic sensitivities would literally explode. When Israel's now Prime Minister Ariel Sharon paid a visit to the Temple Mount—which is Israel's most sacred spot of their three millennia history—he was accused by the Arabs of inciting the recent Palestinian uprising, which to date has cost more than 400 lives. Mind you, he never even entered either of the two Islamic mosques erected over the ruins of those two previous Jewish temples. In fact, he never went near them, let alone leaving any abhorrent Jewish fingerprints on those sacred Muslim shrines!

So what would happen if any real damage were done? You shouldn't require all of three guesses![12]

In an enormous effort to avert any such cataclysmic tidal wave from a sea of violent passions, Israel keeps intense scrutiny over the Temple Mount with a multitude of video cameras to thwart any and all untoward mischief. Mere hearsay of damage—or even presumed desecration to either of the two shrines—could suffice to trigger an uncontrollable eruption. On the other hand, with the current Israeli passions at the boiling point from the incessant and inhumane violence of Palestinian terrorist attacks, bus and roadside bombings, drive-by shootings and wanton slaying of Jewish civilians, the possible success of such vigilante attempts is not at all unrealistic.

Even if it were an earthquake that shook either of those two edifices to pieces, Israel would certainly be blamed. We were in Israel in the summer of 1998 when a smallish earthquake of just over 4 on the Richter Scale shook Israel's Negev region along with the Sinai Peninsula now under Egyptian sovereignty. The following day the Egyptian press blatantly accused Israel of obviously being to blame for the tremor, citing presumed culpability from some sort of underground nuclear experiment they probably had been making!

There is one more portentous feature of the geophysical underpinnings of Old Jerusalem which Someone undoubtedly thought up and engineered eons ago. The Holy City just happens to rest not 50 kilometers from Jordan Rift Valley situated on the mammoth plates of an immensely unstable Syro-African Rift. And who do you suppose might cop the blame for any misadventure there?

But the overall good news is that our above text on the 200 million volunteers never even suggests that this massive militia ever gets anywhere near its goal—and certainly not all of them. Yet bearing in mind the massive expanse of Islam, the bad news is that it surely could well add a tad of trauma to any and all other global well-being en route.

Finally, may we note that the trumpet blast of the sixth

angel is the first trumpet scenario that is not yet measurably underway—even though the potential is well in place. And may we also consider that those first four—if not five—angelically introduced scourges are predominately humanly inaugurated devastation of our God-given planet, with resultant natural repercussions from our own human carelessness, insensitivity and neglect. In the case of the fifth angel, I reckon it's still our own fault. Demons are quite like flies. You open the windows, and they are sure to enter. Keep them shut, and there's no way they can get in. Humankind has quite opened wide the windows into our dwellings of depravity and foreboding haunts of ill repute!

We should note as well that these trumpet events are not exclusively chronologically ordered sequences, but most certainly run and are still running concurrently and with considerable overlap. Let's just take all this information and take a good look around us. What more need I say? Let our unraveling globe speak for itself!

It would be somewhat more than prudent to carefully monitor the events that daily unfold around us in light of the alarming preview presented to us by all six angels—but may we be especially observant of what angel number six is soon to usher in. Would to God that our political leaders had even a fraction of the sensitivity required for decisions in these critical times. The politicians from Caesar onwards have had their opportunities, and it is obvious that it was never intended that they could or would ever be able to deflect humanity from the demise of these days. The real King is what all of creation has desperately been waiting for. And in that context, Jesus repeatedly warned His disciples—which extends to those of us who are disciples today—to keep an eye on the significance of events around us as those long-awaited prophecies unfold:

Be careful, or your hearts will be weighed down with dissipation, drunkenness and the anxieties of life, and that day will close on you unexpectedly like a trap. For it will come upon all those who live on the face of the whole earth. Be always on the watch, and pray that you may be able to escape all that is about to happen, and that you may be able to stand before the Son of Man (Luke 21:34-36).

1 For further discussion see Victor Schlatter, *Where is the Body?* (Shippensburg, PA: Destiny Image Publishers, 1999), pp. 100-101.

2 From Australian Institute for Suicide Research and Prevention, Griffiths University, Mt. Gravatt, Brisbane 4111, Queensland, Australia.

3 "Death Toll in Congo War May Approach 3 Million," *Washington Post,* April 30, 2001.

4 Netanyahu op. cit. pp. 98-99.

5 Ibid. p.102.

6 "Who Will Rescue East Timor?" *Economist,* November 9, 1999. See also "Year 2000 in Review," The Voice of the Martyrs, PO Box 443, Bartlesville, OK, December, 2000.

7 Schlatter, op. cit. pp. 147.

8 "Arafat has $20 million Iraqi Escape Plan," *Jerusalem Post,* Tuesday, March 13, 2001.

9 "Palestinians Offer $2000 for 'Martyrs,' " *Jerusalem Post,* October 7, 2000.

10 "Thousands of Iraqis Drafted into Jerusalem Army," Associated Press cited in *Jerusalem Post,* March 11, 2001; "Iraqis Start Training to Fight for Jerusalem," *Jerusalem Post,* March 12, 2001.

11 Zecharia 12:1-3, 14:1-4; Joel 3:1-2; Isaiah 29:7-8; Mark 13:14-16; and Matthew 24:15-18.

12 Referring to the mosques, Palestinian Authority Minister Abed Rabbo declared, "Trying to touch or to play with the issue of Al Aksa will lead to a religious war...Any attempt to touch even a stone in the Aksa mosque will provoke more than a billion Muslims all over the world." as quoted from "Israel, PA Still Haggling over Jerusalem," *Middle East Digest,* ICEJ News, Jerusalem, September 14, 2000.

CHAPTER 7

Where on Earth Did Heaven Go?

Finally, there is that one last celestial trumpeter with whom to become acquainted:

The seventh angel sounded his trumpet, and there were loud voices in heaven, which said: "The kingdom of the world has become the kingdom of our Lord and of his Christ, and he will reign for ever and ever," (Revelation 11:15).

This final trumpet blast signals the heaven-ordained hand over of power from a disintegrating kingdom of anarchy and increasingly frustrated humanistic systems to the long-promised sovereignty of the King of kings and Lord of lords.

The entire time factor between the sixth and seventh trumpets is unspecified, even cryptically. Who needs to know, anyway? Nevertheless, the events that unfold in Chapter 10 and half of Chapter 11 in the Book of Revelation strongly project a universal confrontation against an uncompromising commitment to the God of Abraham, Isaac and Jacob, which is embedded in Judeo-Christian faith and principles.

Those—both Jew and Gentile—who acknowledge the Hebrew Scriptures as a revelation of the mind and purposes of Almighty God, must ultimately realize that they are destined to a restoration of relationships as they recognize a common

Abba and anticipate a common Jewish Messiah. In Apostle Paul's letter to the believing community in Ephesus, he pens:

> *In reading this, then, you will be able to understand my insight into the mystery of Christ, which was not made known to men in other generations as it has now been revealed by the Spirit to God's holy apostles and prophets. This mystery is that through the gospel the Gentiles are heirs together with Israel, members together of one body, and sharers together in the promise in Christ Jesus* (Ephesians 3:4-6).

Now in the first four chapters of his letter, he repeats the concept of a "mystery" several times, which in the above text he ultimately clarifies quite plainly what it is that has been obscure for so long—the privilege of the Gentiles to also receive a share in the blessings God promised to the Jews through Abraham. And then again in Revelation Chapter 10 we find the final mention of this "mystery" proclaiming that very same restored relationship between both the Jew and Gentile halves of God's extended family in Abraham:

> *But in the days when the seventh angel is about to sound his trumpet,* **the mystery of God will be accomplished**, *just as he announced to his servants the prophets* (Revelation 10:7, emphasis mine).

One really must understand the full context of Paul's letter to the Ephesians to appreciate this. We have been promised common ground for an up-to-now, not-so-common relationship. His eternal plans have been for an ultimately redeemed and unified family, who for millennia had looked from quite different angles on the ground, but ironically, each with an unflinching commitment to the Word of the Living God. If the Scripture is to be accepted as an absolute authority, an ultimate restoration is on the way![1]

Not everyone is going to understand what is happening or why. And, for sure, not everyone is going to appreciate this new arrangement of biblical bedfellows! Never mind. If the Bible, indeed, is true, the Grand Designer will not exactly be searching for anyone else's advice!

The Global Village folks may call both sides of Abraham's restored family—hard-liners, right-wingers, fundamentalists or medieval minds. We all know, of course, that there are not a few loose wires from any and every rightist cause, which curse the planet. But may we never be distracted from the Most High by that minor detail. Let us remind ourselves—and all the rest out there—that the world is not wanting for weirdos on the extreme left as well, who interestingly enough will be far more acceptable to Village life than those who refuse to cooperate on the basis of godly principles.

Therein lies a most fascinating common denominator. It may not be just exactly the same favorite biblical texts that inherently weave together the various strands of the God-fearing, but it will be a rare roll call to one day discover that it is the underlying message of the same Book—the sovereign authority of the one and only creator God of the Universe—that inseparably binds us as children of the same Abba!

Ironically, an equal or even greater binding force betimes is a common adversary. There is a mentality out there that becomes a human sponge for any and all causes from the nutty to the profane, until you try to interest this crowd with divine principles from Above, and then you induce venom by the bucketful. Hell hath no fury like Big Brother scorned.

That interesting little facet from New City Hall might just encourage the God followers to better appreciate each other as well. The bottom line is that there is no way that the no-non-sense, God-honoring Jew nor the truly Bible believing Gentile will edit their Scriptures just to play footsie with the pagans. So if there is such a thing as a God of justice, righteousness and truth, all those of us who take His credentials seriously are not likely to move one centimeter.

I've mentally digested this deep dilemma of 21st century global survival from every point on the compass, and as we have already postulated, if there should happen to be no concerned, involved and innovative God of the Bible out there somewhere, Darwin's "accidents" are in for happening faster on the way out than on the long road in!

In that event, it would be true that the only way for the planet to survive is a Global Village whose main drag is aptly named Middle Road. Ample give and take would have to be the order of the day, and of course if there is no "give," then they "take" the unruly ones with bona fide God-oriented convictions out the back gate and down the hill for a DCC treatment—that is, Divine Conviction Cleansing, which is something like ethnic cleansing but far more "democratic." Anyway, global warming does happen to be a sobering reality—village or no village—while hell freezing up does not happen to be listed in the problem category at the moment, except to underline the probability of success for this Global Village concept in a world that is rapidly disintegrating around us like cotton candy in a tornado.

So these are a few thoughts to reflect on the general essence of what we might expect to encounter during the interim period between the Sixth and Seventh trumpets.[2]

So should the Eternal One still be somewhere in an adjacent galaxy (actually, I just spoke with Him this morning, and did pick up a few positive confirmation signals on the relay), it will be not only a few medieval-minded Judeo-Christian diehards but "the whole of creation" that is up on tippytoes to see it all come together.[3] Sounds like a party!

Included with "all creation"—much of which seems to have a greater appreciation for the Grand Designer than some of the Biped Section has at times—the Alternative Village and every other humanistic hiccup will bow the knee to the strains of Handel's Messiah: "The kingdom of this world has become the kingdom of our Lord and of His Messiah." Well, I for one am getting the genuine goose bump syndrome!

But wait a minute. As thinking people, it's not too difficult to deliberate, "Is this sort of thing really and truly going to happen?" I mean, is it actually, finally going to come off down here on this very planet in real life? After all, humankind has never seen—in these earthbound bones, of course—this kind of celestial celebration. We can talk about it for the great beyond, but not too many of our friends have come back with the "down to earth" information that had hitherto been propelled with presumption.

Down here we do see floods, fire, and famine, which had forever and a day been on the agendas of God's sanctioned seers. We've seen earthquakes and we've seen cyclonic devastation. While on the positive side of the ledger, we've seen—or read about—the seemingly miraculous toppling of despotic tyrants for a triumph of righteousness over evil. We have seen the miraculous in narrow escapes, in dramatic reversals of dire circumstances, in transformed lives, and in physical healing that is well outside any statistical probability. But on the truly celestial side of divine intervention, the feel-it, touch-it, taste-it and test-it-in-the-laboratory stuff has always been a bit out of reach except through personal testimony (which is accepted by some but not by others). This includes supernatural visions, which have yet to be successfully photographed even by modern, technical ingenuity!

What I am saying is that while some of us can see God in everything, others see Him in nothing, which might serve to generate the ever so subtle hesitation to many among us, "Is this all really going to come off the way I had expected?"

Perhaps this is a part of the backtracking that influenced the more theologically enlightened Bible benders from around the 18th century onward to send heaven off into an orbit that can't become too embarrassing should the Ancient of Days somehow have changed His mind. So with fervent faith thus flagging, they eventually got around to biting the bullet and removing the venue of the celestial city from the tangible turf of Mount Zion to the dark side of the moon or somewhere else beyond Galaxy Q (Q is for question mark).

Obviously God's strategic promises to Abraham and His ensuing handiwork in Israel were no longer needed. Nor were His long outmoded prophets, so out they went. That made it easy to keep the Divine at arm's length—a fairly long arm, mind you. That—plus not a few fiascoes by various churches over the ages who presumed themselves to be the Almighty's Press Secretary—launched the inviolable doctrine (or was it principle?) of the "Separation of Heaven and Earth"!

Quoting from my earlier work, "And so it was that a couple hundred years ago when the Bible scholars and devout theologians had a look around Jerusalem and old Judea— never mind that Emperor Hadrian had already renamed it Falistina—they surveyed all this holy dust and wretched rocks and duly surmised that not even the Almighty Himself could resurrect this place!"[4]

And a further quote, "So the theologians of that day might well be forgiven to conclude, therefore, that when the Scriptures tantalize us 800 times with the legacy that is

Jerusalem, and when Isaiah and his fellow prophets spoke delectably of the glorious restoration of Jerusalem, well, they obviously must be talking about somewhere else! So they spiritualized that this new Jerusalem, to which we all aspire, must certainly have its setting in some other realm—say at least a little on the other side of planet Jupiter! They might be forgiven, that is, if their exegesis of the cosmology of the heavens had been a wee bit more realistic, and forgiven if it is determined that sand, rocks, stars, and sky are legitimate substitutes for the Scriptures. I somehow opt for the Word of God."[5]

In the same vein, God's Old Testament prophets, however, knew of, spoke of, and expected no other extra territorial phenomena. They declared what they heard and saw by divine revelation that was to be established in the fullness of time before our very eyes in familiar lines, angles and reality that is plausible enough. Any adventures into the nonmaterial realm were vision-related allegories that only served to reinforce the real thing. They hinted no other inferences than a new Jerusalem—a "heavenly" Jerusalem where Messiah shall reign for a thousand years—which is probably long enough for most of us. All of their writings had a ring of probability that would relate to, and be an extension of, those scenes with which humanity had always been familiar.

So don't actually take it from me. Let's have a good look at what a few of the prophets have told us. Isaiah is probably the most prominent of the lot:

> In the last days the mountain of the LORD's temple will be established as chief among the mountains; it will be raised above the hills, and all nations will stream to it. Many peoples will come and say, "Come, let us go up to the mountain of the LORD, to the house of the God of Jacob. He will

*teach us his ways, so that we may walk in his paths." The
law will go out from Zion, the word of the LORD from
Jerusalem. He will judge between the nations and will
settle disputes for many peoples. They will beat their
swords into plowshares and their spears into pruning
hooks. Nation will not take up sword against nation, nor
will they train for war anymore* (Isaiah 2:2-4).[6]

Prophet Micah pronounces this identical declaration of
Isaiah's in the first three verses of Chapter 4 of his prophecy.
It's word for word the same, so there is no need to repeat it.

Zechariah next to Isaiah was perhaps the foremost prophet
in pinpointing many of the happenings in the Middle East
today, including a number of prophecies dealing with the future of Jerusalem, which are in the formative stage at the moment and which are also certainly soon to come. Some of
these include the kind of Jerusalem that is to be brought into
existence in the final age. Here are two:

*Run, tell that young man, "Jerusalem will be a city
without walls because of the great number of men and live-
stock in it. And I myself will be a wall of fire around it,"
declares the LORD, "and I will be its glory within...."
"Shout and be glad, O Daughter of Zion. For I am
coming, and I will live among you," declares the LORD.
"Many nations will be joined with the LORD in that day
and will become my people. I will live among you and you
will know that the LORD Almighty has sent me to you. The
LORD will inherit Judah as his portion in the holy land and
will again choose Jerusalem"* (Zechariah 2:4-5, 10-12).

And the second one:

This is what the LORD says: "I will return to Zion and dwell in Jerusalem. Then Jerusalem will be called the City of Truth, and the mountain of the LORD Almighty will be called the Holy Mountain." This is what the LORD Almighty says: "I will save my people from the countries of the east and the west. I will bring them back to live in Jerusalem; they will be my people, and I will be faithful and righteous to them as their God" (Zechariah 8:3,7).

Joel has also reflected considerable accuracy about violence, confrontation and the final battle for Jerusalem. He, too, has his bit to proclaim about a new Jerusalem soon to come:

Then you will know that I, the LORD your God, dwell in Zion, my holy hill. Jerusalem will be holy; never again will foreigners invade her. In that day the mountains will drip new wine, all the hills will flow with milk; and all the ravines of Judah will run with water. A fountain will flow out of the LORD'S house and will water the valley of acacias (Joel 3:17-18).

And little known Obadiah (to the average reader) adds his end time bit:

But on Mount Zion will be deliverance; it will be holy, and the house of Jacob will possess its inheritance....Deliverers will go up on Mount Zion to govern the mountains of Esau. And the kingdom will be the LORD's (vs. 17 and 21).

Ezekiel's vision of a future Jerusalem is more than interesting. He left us with nine full chapters at the end of his already lengthy declaration of things to come, describing in the most intricate of measurements, operational functions, design, directional positioning, and all manner of elaborate detail—a temple that is yet to be built! Is this but a symbolic allegory, or is this an actual physical temple ultimately to be erected? Or could it embody both? Bible scholars could argue long and loud (and most certainly do), but the bottom line remains: We will just have to wait and see!

Ezekiel's pronouncement is unique. Never once does he mention Jerusalem or even Mount Zion. The closest he gets is to declare: "All the surrounding area on top of the mountain will be most holy."[7] That's close, but it could be argued that even Mars has mountaintops!

But what Ezekiel does say gets far more territorial—much more earthbound—than physical Jerusalem. In Chapter 47 he speaks of a magnificent and not-so-small river flowing out from under this yet-to-be-observed temple, which is undeniably characteristic of current Jerusalem geography. Moreover, this spectacular stream heads straight for the Dead Sea. Now the abundant springs from the aquifer under the current city is one of the areas worst kept secrets; but all that aside, let's see what Zechariah had to say about that abundant life-giving river that burst forth from underneath the temple and which he saw in his divine vision:

> Then he led me back to the bank of the river. When I arrived there, I saw a great number of trees on each side of the river. He said to me, "This water flows toward the eastern region and goes down into the Arabah, where it enters the Sea. When it empties into the Sea, the water there becomes fresh. Swarms of living creatures will live wherever the river flows. There will be large numbers of fish, because this water flows there and makes the salt

*water fresh; so where the river flows everything will live.
Fishermen will stand along the shore; from En Gedi to En
Eglaim there will be places for spreading nets. The fish will
be of many kinds—like the fish of the Great Sea. But the
swamps and marshes will not become fresh: they will be
left for salt"* (Ezekiel 47:6-11).

Now that sounds like very literal places to most of us.
Moreover, for those of us who know Israel, En Gedi is a current
kibbutz on the periphery of the Dead Sea, the Arabah (or
Arava as it is spelled in modern Hebrew) is the general Dead
Sea Valley and is an inescapable reality on all the present maps
of Israel. Moreover, Ezekiel further describes the boundaries of
the entire land with such readily recognizable mile markers as
Egypt, Damascus and the Mediterranean Sea in the remainder
of Chapter 47, and cements the identity of the terrain with a
number of additional earthbound sites in Chapter 48.

So who in the *world* ever had the audacity to shift this divinely ordered venue to outer space? I suggest we come back
down to *earth* in the matter.

Before we leave our Ezekiel references, why did he not
mention Zion or Jerusalem? Since there was a name revision
for the celestial city already on the agenda, perhaps he was divinely directed to begin with the new name right then and
there:

*And the name of the city from that time on will be: THE
LORD IS THERE* (Ezekiel 48:35b).[8]

Finally, in the last two chapters of the Book of Revelation
in the New Testament, the memorable heavenly visions of John
are indelibly etched into the consciousness of most Christians.
Artists have endeavored to capture the celestial grandeur of the

city on canvas over the last two millennia whether or not they had to be committal to position it upon a fluffy cloud or leave it there where it was on *terra firma*. The great composer George Frederick Handel had no such problem in grappling with the geography. He just hung in there with the Scriptures, and his angelic anointing added the divine dimension without having to touch on difficult real estate decisions.

Unfortunately, studying only Chapters 21 and 22 in Revelation leaves one a bit "up in the air" as to where this city will eventually be located—unless, of course, one seriously notes that John tells us that this new Jerusalem *comes down* out of heaven, which—as even aeronautical engineers will readily understand—is not quite the same as up.[9] Let us remember that John had all of his foundational information from the Old Testament prophets, and he himself was one of the initial pillars of the church. Those who dare jettison John's insights have wandered too far down the garden path!

In fact, John's vision was not a "garden path" but a river with trees on either side, which bears a striking relationship with the river that Ezekiel tells us about in his Chapter 47. Obviously John had a bit more confidence in the ancient Hebrew prophets than did some of our more recent theologians!

Now in our day, with increasing facts on the ground in and around Jerusalem, we hold our breath as the Ancient of Days ticks off more and more of His age-old prophetic warnings as they stir from over 2000 years of slumber and, slowly but surely, come to life. Who dare deny the Scriptures that the final restoration of an old Jerusalem is long overdue? Her presently dirty stones, less than sanitized streets and blood drenched history await with countless tears her promised redemption. As I observe her today, that cannot be far off. Nor were the prophets who told us of these days nearly three millennia ago.

That, of course, is all very interesting, but what, indeed, is the major insight afforded by this chapter? As we probe overall, what can be done with a God who impudently insists on interfering in the private affairs of grown men and women? It would appear that a society that has long come of age can quite nicely steer their own ships, thank you very much!

With all the trouble she has caused with the Arabs, Jerusalem is the last place any calculating humanist would want to establish our Global Village. London is too foggy; Los Angeles is already too big. But there's Paris, and there's Brussels. Geneva is perhaps the best bet, but then there's even New York City!

Indeed, there is a bit of confrontation already in the air, but I'm ready. The Scriptures have already clearly told us whose venue will win the day, and that should make us all more than ready—goose bumps and all! Courage surges to the fore to confront those Global Village gendarmes who will bend over backwards to any kooky cause, except for an Eternal Creator God who happens to bring His own agenda to the table, with the not so subtle reminder that the I AM still is.

Okay, Big Brother, where did you hide those wimpy lions?

1 For a detailed discussion on this aspect of Ephesians, see Schlatter, op. cit. pp. 33-44.

2 Ibid. The allegory in Revelation Chapter 11 is dealt with in considerable detail in Chapters 9 (Two Olive Trees) and 10 (Eschatology According to James).

3 Romans 8:19 as translated by J.B. Phillips, *The New Testament in Modern English* (London: Macmillan, 1965).

4 Schlatter, op. cit. p. 61

5 Ibid. p.62, paragraph 5.

6 An additional longer and even more detailed quote from Isaiah is 65:17-25.

7 See Ezekiel 43:12.

8 See also Isaiah 12:6, 24:23; Jeremiah 3:17; Joel 3:21; Revelation 3:12, 21:3.

9 See Revelation 21:2.

CHAPTER 8
Along with Tribulation, *The* Is a Four-letter Word!

From time to time we may have well-meaning folk who will inform us that God will never let His people suffer, but will eventually take us all out of here to a celestial space station that will make NASA look like a bunch of preschool kids with Legos™. Aside from the NASA bit, this is all very comforting, but certainly a startling new twist since Bible times. Not sure what happened to Jesus' dire warnings for the end of days?:

> *And you will be brought before kings and governors, and all on account of my name. This will result in your being witnesses to them.... You will be betrayed even by parents, brothers, relatives and friends, and they will put some of you to death. All men will hate you because of me. But not a hair of your head will perish. By standing firm you will gain life (Luke 21:12-13; 16-19).*

Obviously, there are those among us who presume to have the credentials to clarify to the rest of us what He really meant to say. In reality, for all who take the Scriptures seriously, it does seem that before any abrupt exits, a few more politically correct objections to our Judeo-Christian faith may well be surfacing, and that not too far around the corner! Which, of course, instead of day-dreaming, should serve to make us increasingly watchful as the globe shrinks ominously around us.

When I was a young fellow, I was given to believe that some add-on good news was that none of this terrible stuff Jesus warned about could ever happen to us believers at this late date, or even take place around us. Perhaps many of us were introduced to this rather recent-in-time "immunity theory," which is not yet 200 years old. However, should this neo-conjecture of painless passage indeed be true, we've never been left with a legitimate reason why our Lord ever said it in the first place? Never mind. Let's not let the fine print ever get in the way of a best-selling hypothesis!

Anyway, as the speculation goes, when Jesus spoke of "great tribulation, such as never was, not since the beginning of the world to this time, no, nor ever shall be,"[1] what He really meant to say was that this tribulation would be exactly seven years long, and that true believers could promptly forget about it because they wouldn't be here anyway. To the contrary, they would, in fact, be caught up in a heavenly orbit during this distressful period, having a party all on their own!

Moreover, the thus-far unbelieving Jews—among others who had known better but failed to declare their faith—will be left behind during this period to be "taught a lesson." Nevertheless, if during this seven-year period of tribulation, some of those who missed out were to die a martyr's death—as the theory goes—they could still come good after this seven-year hiatus had run its course. We are not told, unfortunately, whether a second party will be thrown for those faithful martyrs who came in late and severely suffered for it. Not a few blanks on the non-biblical side of the hypothesis remain to be filled in!

Now Jesus was citing almost verbatim from the prophet

Daniel, and to be sure some parts of this novel idea above are very much from the Bible. There *will be* tribulation such as never was nor ever will be. There *will be* a departure of the saints from an evil, degenerate society at some point in time, which for ready reference has been labeled as a "rapture" by more recent theologians. But beyond that, the jumbled juxtaposition of the events with ensuing non-biblical assumptions become as suspect as a seven-dollar bill. If this is what Jesus truly meant, one wonders why He didn't say so, and why He left it to the 19th century experts—to be amplified in the 20th century—to spring upon us the real inside scoop? Sorry, but the original words of Jesus are clear enough for all those who want to hear them, and this is *not* what He told us.

In a nutshell, here is what is wrong with the I-won't-be-around theory:

1. Nowhere in the Scriptures are we told that the period of tribulation that both Jesus and Daniel spoke of has a limited time frame of seven years. This novel deduction gave essence to the now ultra-popular term, "The Trib." Neither Jesus nor Daniel even hinted in this direction. Tribulation, most certainly, but not "The" Tribulation, which would suggest the status of a singular identifiable event with a presumed time frame. *The* is not from the Bible. Check it out!

2 The brainstorm of a seven-year period comes from piecing together other cryptic comments from Daniel's end of the age prophecies. Whether Daniel's prophetic seven years, three-and-a-half years or even 70 years are taken literally, figuratively or otherwise, facts on the ground from Auschwitz to Israel's Day of Independence on May 14, 1948, to the liberation of Jerusalem on June 4, 1967, down to the soon to erupt final battle for Jerusalem[2] negates this kind of speculation. After all, these prophecies are focused on Israel, remember, and not on London, Paris or Washington.

3. The first expression of a "rapture" type event is in Chapter 14 of the prophet Zechariah as he foretells the Lord's rescue of Jerusalem from her adversaries in the end of days. And "all His holy ones," at that point in time, appear with Him in the heavens above the Mount of Olives. Jesus then reinforces this promise in detail three times while seated with His disciples on that identical Mount of Olives. Long afterward, Paul relays the very same scenario to the believers, first in Corinth and lastly in Thessalonica—this final reference being the only one most people are ever told about. But no reasonable scholars dare work from the New Testament backwards, but from the initial reference in the Old Testament to the culmination of events in the New![3]

4. Finally, anyone studying the words of Jesus in Matthew Chapter 24, Mark Chapter 13 and Luke Chapter 21 must find the proposition most absurd that Bible believers will be required to face no challenge and no persecution near the end of days. The affluence of a Western society with a bathroom shelf full of pain killers has obviously made great strides, not only in medicine, but in theological understanding as well!

In reinforcement of what we have just said, I suggest you have a look at *Foxes Book of Martyrs*.[4] Only after having soberly pondered what the faithful of the early church endured, may we begin to reflect seriously on the sufferings of the saints in our very day as faithfully reported in accurate Christian news services. Bulletins from worldwide mission agencies abound. Have you heard what is happening to the God-fearing in Sudan, Indonesia, West Africa, Nepal, Iran and throughout many of the Arabic nations? Perhaps you might also look up the good people who publish the more contemporary *Voice of Martyrs* to keep abreast of what is going on these days in the real world.[5]

Nor dare we forget the Jews who by biblical mandate and God-ordered convictions have settled on their own land in the Judea, Samaria and Gaza of their ancient inheritance, only to be menaced by mortar shells falling upon their homes, farms and rural communities. Or can we hide our eyes to the almost daily drive-by shootings on Israeli roads and at Jewish school buses—or the detonation of massive terrorist bombs in Israel's public markets, city centers, shopping malls and public buses.

Internationally led by CNN and the BBC—and slavishly followed by their hordes of less than honest TV and print media compatriots worldwide—the global media usually forgets to call to our attention these tragic Jewish victims, since their politically correct "crusade of justice" seems to become far more preoccupied with casualties among the Islamic terrorists, the Johnny-come-lately Palestinian rioters and murderers who since the 1920s have been venting their wrath upon the "evil Zionists" (read: Bible-committed Jews). Obviously, checking back into historical accuracy of the one-liner claims and innuendoes in today's media broadcasts is a non-starter![6] This present round-the-world scenario of anti-Christian, anti-Semitic sensitivities gives us a reasonably good window into the quality and the virtue of the judicial system of our now less than inviting Village-to-be.

Indeed the righteous do suffer, and they always did. On the other hand, this does not necessarily suggest that all of the faithful at the end of days are going to be mercilessly destined to the guillotine, the flames, or the firing squad. In the biblical record, the faithful Jeremiahs who escaped the wrath of the evil systems of their day usually seemed to outnumber the John the Baptizers who were beheaded. Know your Bible, believe your God and thereby take courage!

God forbid that I propel anyone off into a trauma trip

since that is no more scriptural than our opening statements regarding those who would injudiciously project a painless dreamland escape. Our purposes throughout are to get our eyes off of what is fanciful, false and phony and get a measurement on what is actually happening under our very noses to enable us to proceed—eyes wide open—and with not a little wisdom.

Certainly there will always be some adversity, and surely there will be those who will be required to pay the supreme price. But the Eternal One always has had and always will have a majestic kaleidoscope of rescue channels for His faithful. Kings and prophets, apostles or nobodies like Rahab the prostitute, were all within a hair of the sword, but God delivered them by a mile. Not only do these accounts make some of the most exciting challenges in the Scriptures, but they indelibly underline the ultimate intention of the Almighty and His walk with His friends. We are steered from the pit, neither with ecclesiastical formulae nor sanctified "problem" insurance, but *by intimacy with our God*. In addition to maintaining a perpetual hot line, our God has a lot of umbrellas of various sizes and styles, custom-made for any and all who are ready to trust Him.[7]

Now, just to make sure we have it all together, let's take a quick overview of these last three chapters beginning with the Seven Angels with Seven Trumpets in Revelation Chapters 8 through 11. John the Apostle, who was called upon to share the Lord's final vision with us, also presents us with three other sets of sevens. A vision of Seven Seals are reported first, primarily in Chapters 6 and 7. Then there were the voices of the Seven Thunders in Revelation Chapter 10, which still happen to be on hold in the archives of the Almighty since John was told with no uncertainty not to give away any clues just yet. And then there are the Seven Bowls of God's wrath ominously depicted in Revelation Chapter 16—a bit scary, those.

So why all these sevens? Seven is a fairly popular number in God's crypto-numerology and generally represents the entirety or completeness of a significant programmed event. I would guess that should be enough background to satisfy our needs at the moment. I don't want to get too far afield as we proceed to compare the long range agenda of the Ancient of Days with a few opposing blueprints for the New World Order, Inc.

There are a few scholars who see the seals, the trumpets and the bowls as three allegorical presentations of the same sequence of events. I don't. First, the trumpets seem to be genuinely humanly instigated. The bowls seem definitely to have a "Designed in Outer Space" stamp on them.

True, there are so-so parallels between a few of the steps in each of the seven sequences. But the more deeply we merge into the end of the action—including the final battle for Jerusalem—the more clearly it becomes that these several prophesied series of events cannot be one and the same.

We're not going to go into the fine print in these matters, which is quite aside from my purposes in these pages. In fact, so much fine print has already been processed by would-be expositors on the intrigues of Revelation, we should by now have alphabet soup enough to feed all the world's hungry. The real truth is that none of us mortals genuinely have a handle on all this fine print anyway. By and large, we were challenged not to resolve riddles, but to watch—that is, to keep our eyes open to all that is falling into place around us. And this has been my goal throughout.

Therefore quite in brief, the Seven Seals would appear to scan history over the last 2000 years. In fact, these seals have a very fascinating parallel, if not reinforcement, with seven of the major points Jesus made to His disciples in Matthew Chapter 24 when He gave them the lowdown on what things they were to expect in both the near and the then distant future. For example, He begins with false messiahs, which trigger a resemblance of conquerors on white horses as it were, who have arisen to play God over the last two millennia. He proceeds to wars and rumors of wars, famine and deathly plagues. These events are commonly associated with the red horse, black horse and pale horse envisioned in the following three seals and which do, quite characteristically, reflect these readily recognized miseries of mankind, which have spanned the 20 centuries from Jesus' discourse until now. And, finally, that which currently lies on the table—betrayal and martyrdom, a major power outage in the universe, and the final countdown up until the day of the Lord follows in their wake.

This reinforcement of Matthew Chapter 24 by the Seven Seals of Revelation is a little more than impressive. Nevertheless, the passing recognition of it is sufficient for our purposes here. Much of it is already history, but with the paradox that this history of misery, deprivation and bloodshed still lingers with us until this very day. Only the celestial lights of the heavens have yet to go out before the lights of Glory are finally turned on!

But the Seven Trumpets are much more specific to our overall purposes. Who dare deny the rotting fruits of humankind's irresponsibility in taking care of the planet God gave us as characterized by the first four angels. And all the while, selfish indifference to the man-made disasters already upon us—not to mention the ominous threats and rhetoric for non-conventional warfare soon to surface in the Middle East—remind us it can only get worse.

What, pray tell, programmed the worldwide demonic epidemic that emanates from our urban slums outward to the "decent people" (read: "the affluent, the indifferent and the greedy"), other than our own human insensitivity to the deprived, the downtrodden and the helpless at our gates? Like flies to a manure pile, demons flock to humanity's failures. This was quite of our own making, and the Almighty had nothing to do with lighting the fuse.

Then what of the 200 million-strong (undoubtedly Islamic) militia emanating from the environs of the Euphrates River as signaled by angel number six? And what of Islam—vehemently opposed to the Judeo-Christian tradition—who is now more than determined to make good its declaration to take an Allah-assured grasp on the 21st century by year 2050 or sooner? How in the world did it get this far? Could it be that the Western World's appetite for oil was—and still is—far greater than her appetite for truth? The aftermath of the Seven Angels—the pay-out of humanity's apostasy and self-centered priorities—is well and truly upon us.

Last of all, there are those wretched bowls of God's wrath as described in detail in Chapter 16 of Revelation. I mean, this is a scenario when we *do* want to be somewhere else! What about those seven horrendous Bowls of Wrath? Please carefully note that these cataclysmic plagues are chronologically listed at some point after the Kingdom of God and His Messiah is begun midway into Chapter 11 of Revelation—the precise center of the Apocalypse, which John has passed on to warn us. The Seven Trumpets reflect the demise that humanity has brought down upon its own head. With the Seven Bowls of Wrath, it is God's turn to judge a rebellious and apostate globe. Please note that these final seven plagues take place *outside* the reconstructed Jerusalem, well beyond the pale of the City of the Great King.

Picking up and finalizing the thread from our previous chapter, if the ancient prophets are to be believed—and Jesus certainly believed and constantly quoted them—then the King of kings is destined to assume His new office on Mount Zion in the heart of a divinely restored Jerusalem, and a new worldwide era of God-selected leadership—Messiahship to be precise—takes over the planet.

In both Old and New Testaments there is more than clear understanding that life continues apace in Jerusalem after the long-awaited Kingdom of God comes into its own.

Then the survivors from all the nations that have attacked Jerusalem will go up year after year to worship the King, the LORD Almighty, and to celebrate the Feast of Tabernacles. If any of the peoples of the earth do not go up to Jerusalem to worship the King, the LORD Almighty, they will have no rain (Zechariah 14:16-17).

And in the New Testament:

I saw the Holy City, the new Jerusalem, coming down out of heaven from God, prepared as a bride beautifully dressed for her husband. And I heard a loud voice from the throne saying, "Now the dwelling of God is with men, and he will live with them. They will be his people, and God himself will be with them and be their God. Outside are the dogs, those who practice magic arts, the sexually immoral, the murderers, the idolaters and everyone who loves and practices falsehood (Revelation 21:2-3; 22:15).[8]

Moreover, it appears that the real estate in New Jerusalem City might be a bit more up-market than in the New World

Order Villas, and it might be just a bit more relaxed *inside* those comforting if not impressive walls—like no nasty buckets of divine wrath.

However, if anyone has a problem with this conclusion, he has two options.

1. Investigate a few more Scriptures yourself to evaluate what Jesus believed and taught about the veracity of the prophets. If it's good enough for the Son of Man, what might be our problem?

2. The alternative is to get a bid in for a cute little three bedroom pad in the Global Village where you will be guaranteed no interference from Above or even from kooky prophets from below. But as we were cautioned earlier on in Chapter 4, on any and all NWO deals, one must be sure he has thoroughly scrutinized all the fine print. Are you sure you really want to buy a used car from those guys—not to mention a new house!

1 See Daniel 12:1; Matthew 24:21; Mark 13:19.

2 "Arafat Stirs Islamic Furor over Jerusalem," *Middle East Digest,* August 28, 2000; "PA's Meddain Issues Threat of Regional War against Israel," *Israel Wire,* June 26, 2000; "Teheran Bash Calls for Jihad to Crush Israel," *Middle East Digest: ICEJ News,* April 25, 2001.

3 This explicitly follows the hermeneutical principal of first reference: See Zechariah 14:1-5; Matthew 24:30-31; Mark 13:26-27; Luke 21:27-28; 1 Corinthians 15:51-52; 1 Thessalonians 4:16-17.

4 John Foxe, *Foxes Book of Martyrs* (Boston, MA: Whitaker House, March 1991).

5 See "Year 2000 in Review," op. cit. December, 2000.

6 Demographic statistics from the British Mandate reveal that the majority of Arab population flowed into Palestine after WW 1 and even up to the formation of the State of Israel in 1948. See Peters, op. cit. Chapter 12, "A Hidden Factor in Western Palestine: Arab In-Migration," pp. 234-268 and Chapter 13 "A Hidden Movement: Illegal Arab Immigration," pp. 269-295, and Barry Chamish, *The Last Days of Israel: Why the "Palestinians Have No Right to a State"* (Tempe, AZ: Dandelion Books, 2001), pp. 112-114.

7 For a unique scenario see: Schlatter, op. cit. Chapter 10 "Eschatology According to James."

8 See additional New Testament references in Luke 21:24b; Hebrews 11:10, 13:14; Revelation 11:2, 21:10,14,16

CHAPTER 9

The Pronoun Problem

Back in the 1970s when the Holy Spirit renewal of those days was gaining momentum to sweep the globe, my wife and I were correspondingly blessed with spiritual dimensions hitherto unknown to us. In fact, some days prior to one memorable—and ever since indelible—encounter with the Most High, I had been plodding my way through the struggle of translating the book of Ephesians into the Waola language, one of the some 750 tribal tongues of Papua New Guinea. I had been about three chapters into the translation, but due to the heightened sensitivity from that intimate touch of the Almighty, the hitherto leanness of my rough draft of those initial three chapters became stark reality. After jettisoning those some two weeks of my own human efforts to File 13, I began translating Ephesians all over again at an exciting new level of inspiration.

I still have a bit of a nostalgic tug for those times, and not the least was singing those songs straight out of the *King James Bible*, put to music with those simple but catchy chorus tunes of the day. Fantastic way to learn Scripture, it was. The words just don't slip away. The humbling thing was to find out that the ancient Hebrews had been praising the Lord with psalms like this ever since the time of King David, some 3000 years ago. Young David reportedly received the inspiration during his Judean Desert Prep School in Ovine-ology, but unfortunately he could only read and write in Hebrew. For all those not learned in monarchy matters, David surfaced into the king business a fair few years before there ever was such a regal protégé as King James who—as far as my research can detect—was raised up specifically to translate David's verses into the king's English! To get serious, King James poetry is *almost* as beautiful as Hebrew.

Anyway, that was just a bit of reminiscing. What we really want to talk about are those Scripture songs of the 60s and 70s, namely one special favorite, "Our God Reigns." You probably know it and appreciate it yourself.

Sadly, that wasn't the name of that chorus back then. Someone has long since changed it. The original name was "Your God Reigns," which, with some small poetic license, was lifted straight from the message of Isaiah the Prophet :

> *How beautiful on the mountains are the feet of those who bring good news, who proclaim peace, who bring good tidings, who proclaim salvation, who say to Zion, "**Your** God reigns!" Listen! Your watchmen lift up their voices; together they shout for joy. When the LORD returns to Zion, they will see it with their own eyes. Burst into songs of joy together, you ruins of Jerusalem, for the LORD has comforted his people, he has redeemed Jerusalem. The LORD will lay bare his holy arm in the sight of all the nations, and all the ends of the earth will see the salvation of our God* (Isaiah 52:7-10, emphasis mine).

That initial version—adapted to music—had all those neat verses about the feet on the mountains that brought good news, watchmen on the walls of Jerusalem, redemption of Zion and the Lord comforting His people. I mean, that's exactly what the original text was all about. It's about Redemption on a very expansive scope.

Not anymore. Someone dropped all that old Jerusalem Scripture and worked up some new lyrics to be a bit more relevant to the contemporary sentiment of the times. And then they changed the title to "*Our* God Reigns."

Do you see what happened? The original message was a prophecy of encouragement to an entire city. Not just any city, mind you, but *the* City! It was the city—indeed much more than a city—which is referred to at least 20 times in Deuteronomy alone as, "The place where the Lord your God [chose] as a dwelling for His Name."[1] The original Scripture says, in effect, "Don't worry, Jerusalem"—and any and all who are associated with her, including you and I—"your King is coming."

But He has by now been so long in coming—at least, in coming back to restore Jerusalem—who has time these busy days to bother with some detached and long ago promised Redemption Center? We have enough of our own problems, not to mention a fairly heavy agenda right here. Jerusalem is totally irrelevant to where I'm at now.

So we shift the focus of the chorus a bit to make it fit our own personal circumstances. Or is it because the original message was never really fully comprehended? Or both?

Unfortunately, in these hectic times, God no longer "belongs" to the prophetic city—no more is He the collective hope of a crushed humanity where the initial directive was, "beginning at Jerusalem" Well, yes, I suppose in a sense He still does, but at the moment the most important thing is, "*I'm* hurting. He belongs to *me*." He belongs to *us*. "*Our* God Reigns!" So they changed it, and the faithful barely blinked.

Looks like we have a pronoun problem.

Reminds me of C. S. Lewis' classic window into the selfish side of our psyche when he illustrated humankind's "progressive" reasoning in the immortal *Screwtape Letters*: "...my boots...my dog...my wife...my God.."[2]

Your God reigns, Jerusalem! Even though one ought to understand that this would naturally include ourselves in the ultimate redemptive promise as well, it doesn't exactly excite the individualistic human spirit as much as *my* God—*our* God. And in the same almost unconscious vein, it follows directly that it is a very comforting, self-centered, and yes, humanistic feeling that the Almighty might even fit quite nicely into my clutch purse or shirt pocket. What were we doing all during the time that human society—including religious systems—went about systematically downsizing our God to a bit of personal property? Having parties? Playing church? Rewriting songs that better fit our moods?

But this is hardly a faux pas preserved for our present time. Let's look at the premier performance:

> *The woman said to the serpent, "We may eat fruit from the trees in the garden, but God did say, 'You must not eat fruit from the tree that is in the middle of the garden, and you must not touch it, or you will die.'"*

> *"You will not surely die," the serpent said to the woman. "For God knows that when you eat of it your eyes will be opened, and you will be like God, knowing good and evil"* (Genesis 3:2-4).

As I said earlier, there are two reasons for everything—a good reason and the real reason. A good reason for our problem might be pronouns, but the bottom line is mankind's penchant for competing with the Almighty. When old snake eyes convinced Eve she was going to be like God, he had our first mama hooked!

Ironically, Abba wants us to be like Him, but not quite by our own cunning. He has His own preferred parenting program, which more than welcomes our cooperation, but He hardly yearns for our improvement to His agenda. And we do have to admit, He does have a slight edge with experience!

The first commandment given to Moses sets the program straight—"No other Gods before me."[3] That includes gold-crafted bulls and hand-carved statues from days of yore. And transliterated for today's more sophisticated up-market crowd, it involves everything from affluence, power and big bucks to the much more subtle appetites of incognito humanism.

Dare we concur that humanism is anything but a fig leaf to cover the arrogance—or is it ignorance—of a society that presumes itself to have come of age? One must recall the tongue-in-cheek comment of Mark Twain reflecting on his youthful years between 18 and 21. He was amazed how much his father had learned during that period! Our progressively humanistic society is like a grand conglomeration of highly programmed and technically learned university students, shouting slogans, marching with placards and protesting political issues far beyond their levels of genuine maturity. Are we truly becoming wiser? Or is it merely an extension—perhaps a final crescendo—of primitive Cain shaking his grubby fist at a Creator with whom he cannot agree?

In fact, rebelling against God or competing with God has little difference except that the latter can be much more easily disguised with social—including religious—camouflage. In Chapter 3 we have already touched on the first organized effort to build a society that would require help from no one, and least of all from the "otherness" of outer space. Let's have another look at that text in Genesis on the Tower of Babel in a bit more detail:

> As men moved eastward, they found a plain in Shinar and settled there. They said to each other, "Come, let's make bricks and bake them thoroughly." They used brick instead of stone, and tar for mortar. Then they said, "Come, let us build ourselves a city, with a tower that reaches to the heavens, so that we may make a name for ourselves and not be scattered over the face of the whole earth." But the LORD came down to see the city and the tower that the men were building. The LORD said, "If as one people speaking the same language they have begun to do this, then nothing they plan to do will be impossible for them" (Genesis 11:2-6).

Considerable symbolism is incorporated in this simple, but at the same time profound, account. A tower is the ancient symbol of authority, overview, command and power. The stones and clay, El Shaddai's "so-so efforts" of creation, were replaced with superior materials of their own design—brick and tar—which as you can see may well serve their interest far better. But their ultimate intention was "A *name* for ourselves" so they would not be scattered and ultimately weakened by any other Force (or forces) of the universe.

Certainly the technology of improving on building blocks from atoms or molecules to cement or steel for skyscrapers is hardly an affront to the King of the Universe. In fact, He specifically put man in charge of His creation and encouraged him to subdue the world placed at his feet.[4] Moreover,

Solomon the Wise continually extols us to pursue wisdom, knowledge and understanding throughout the book of Proverbs. But motives are everything, while the implied insolence of Babel Builders, Inc., is not much. A name for ourselves, indeed!

There are three arenas of life where mortals make fools of themselves under the observant eye of the Eternal One: Their fill of the flesh, the fill of their pockets and an exalted name.[5] And possibly the lust for a name to be honored above one's peers is the greatest appetite of all. That ambition knows no status boundaries, whether the one who yearns to ascend, himself, happens to be high up or far down on the relative social ladder of his personal circumstances. Just give me a mountain to conquer—the easiest perhaps being one of my fellow human beings who is most conveniently near at hand.

One of the earliest focal points of the Israelite community as they emerged from their slavery in Egypt was the sanctity of the name of Almighty God. The third commandment on the slate is perhaps a composite of the first two:

> You shall not misuse the name of the LORD your God, for the LORD will not hold anyone guiltless who misuses his name (Exodus 20:7).

In fact, Orthodox Jews to this very day will never dare to utter God's sacred name lest by some shade of irreverence in their manner, they be found guilty. What do they say? How do they pray? To avoid any offense, the simplest expression in Hebrew is *Ha Shem*: "The Name."

The evident lesson is that we don't need a big name—and particularly so when it is gained in crushing another. Our Abba's name should be quite enough.

*And whatever you do, whether in word or deed, do it all in
the name of the Lord Jesus, giving thanks to God the
Father through him* (Colossians 3:17).

Our tower of Babel is an anti-God mindset that has obviously been around for quite a while. Undoubtedly, with the shrinking of the globe, mass communication has taught us the latest details of political correctness while the Internet demonstrated the fine-tuning. That humanly independent mindset of Babel has gained not a little momentum during the final half of the last century and by now has gone exponential.

So where does competition first enter into the arena of life? The first sibling rivalry is recorded in the Bible in the account of brothers Cain and Abel, with the ultimate and untimely murder of Abel the younger.[6]

The only families where sibling rivalry seems not to occur are those where there are no kids! Even an unwitting and immature parent can create a minimal substitute in a one-child home. In my own experience, I got along reasonably well with one of my two siblings, but with the other we did unabated battle well into our teenage years.

In the years that followed, my wife and I had four beautiful children of our own. In retrospect we realized we had nurtured—perhaps in our own lack of vision—two pairs of juvenile rivals. Adulthood and maturity ordinarily terminate these childhood battles, but unfortunately others are only grudgingly surrendered at the grave. Darwin tried to tell us that we are but residue from the survival of the fittest. Whether wittingly into Darwin or not, it appears that we have gleefully grabbed up that baton for ourselves, and we run for all we are worth in the welcomed opportunity of getting to thump our nearest would-be challenger.

Meanwhile, the Bible has presented to us that we were designed as one human family with a common Father to follow. Nowhere in the Scriptures from Moses' God-given laws of human relationships through to the New Testament fruits of the Spirit, will we ever find competition a virtue or rivalry anything but a vice. How could "comfortable Christian lifestyle" ever get sucked so far down the sordid tube of humanistic behavior?

The norm of accepted Western lifestyle has finally become a mad scramble pitted against someone else—known or unknown, identified or not—perhaps a singular adversary or possibly a collective threat. Is this what our Maker designed it all to be? Who turned a corner?

The Ancient Greek philosophers, first of all, clarified to the world that there never was a Maker at all! Mythical gods to be "milked"? If you so choose, why not? But the real god was man himself. And then they gave us those "valuable" Western insights of "democratic" rule that capitalized on exalting the inherent "god-powers" of humanity, underlining the supremacy of the individual freedoms of choice. Did you think that "human rights" was a new concept dreamed up by the United Nations? Sorry.

Thus, the worldview of the ancient Hellenists clashed headlong with the earlier Hebraic concepts of a Creator God who cared for His extended family, and they in turn cared for one another by law—His law. And may we make no mistake about it, the sovereign Lawgiver was in full control. Therefore the Hellenistic innovation ultimately (who were these retarded Hebrews anyway?) precipitated drastic changes in Western thought and culture. While giving lip service to an increasingly distant Deity, the individual began to be more and more relaxed in being king of his own hill. And, ironically, this Hellenistic syncretism eventually surfaced both among some of the Jews in the Maccabean period of the 2nd century BC, and throughout even more of the early church fathers in the 3rd and 4th centuries of the Christian era. And if we take a few moments to look around us, it has obviously been gaining a fair bit of added momentum ever since.[7]

Thus we have the watershed where Judeo-Christian "hard-liners" emanate. We acknowledge the Bible and its divine authority over Plato, Pericles, Aristotle or any other contestants. And that bedrock absolute significantly falls on both sides of the Judeo-Christian declaration of an Almighty God whose claim to sovereignty is non-negotiable.

Meanwhile, the more affluent those became whose eyes had drifted westward to this "improved" system of individual enterprise, the more the "little god-within-me kings" started popping up like mushrooms. And the big kings got even bigger while the non-kings—i.e., the losers—just got buried and forgotten. Or was their doom perhaps sealed in the reverse order? And for the winners, it felt so good to be on top, it could in no way be that far out of the will of God. Obviously this fantastic concept of improving overall achievement by humanistic oriented competition with one's fellows never, ever occurred to the Almighty, or He might have even proposed it Himself!

Yes, I know, this is not for you because you're anything but rich. You're one of those little guys—or gals—that keeps getting stomped on—*battlers* we call them in Australia. And you know what it's like to get squished. Excuse me. Remember the bit of statistics we had back in Chapter 3 titled The Fortunate Few? If you are literate and can read these pages, you're in the top 30% of global society. If your home does not have a grass roof and a dirt floor, and does have an inside toilet, you are in the top 20%. And if you own a computer or have a university degree you have hit the top 1% of the planet. No matter how tough it is at times, there are a lot more people living downstairs. So most of us have a dual role to play throughout life—both as prince and pauper—so these insights are a two-way street. The God of the Bible addresses both roles. The god of the Hellenistic mentality addresses only himself.

We can hardly involve our Greek mentors with entrepreneur Cain's private initiative to eliminate the presumed threat of his younger brother. Therefore we can only conclude that the pagan Greeks were hardly the first to get a patent on human "freedom" over against the more caring Hebraic communal view of responsibility to the extended family. It would, in fact, appear that it took the Greeks far longer to come to the conclusion of the "final solution" than it did Cain![8]

Nevertheless, Greek culture taught us lots of other neat tricks about individual freedoms that led us to even "higher" ambitions like unbridled freedom of speech and nebulous—if not dubious—civil liberties. It shouldn't take too many doctoral degrees to conclude that with over 6 billion people now on the planet, a few of these individual "rights" are going to have to intersect with someone else's "rights," beginning perchance with the guy next door!

Of course the legal people have already thought this one through, and are making a killing with their "rights" to get rich. Constitutional democracy has replaced the bedrock morals and values of Moses. (If I read my Bible correctly, it wasn't even Moses who came up with the ideas—he was only the courier!) So in the new age of a new world under new order, we can now create legislate-as-you-go situational ethics—political correctness come of age—and the whole ship is now bobbing without anchor in the wild seas of political craftiness. Scary, indeed, but in one more sober moment of truth, WE ARE THERE!

Nor dare we neglect to bow down in gratitude to our Hellenistic innovators. They have now offered us a "more natural soil" of humanistic thinking—"mother nature" has little use for bedrock—thus generating a self-satisfied and self-sufficient society that once the memorials to the gods are safely in museums, we need no other help.[9]

But hold on. That same Greek culture did give us the Olympics, did it not? No problems there! Like all Australians I was a bit pleased with our athletes in the recent Sydney Games and was more than proud of our aboriginal Kathy Freeman in her outstanding achievements, her excellent spirit, her representation of her people. Now that *was* good.

Indeed, there is a lot of good sportsmanship in this Greek gift to the world and that's the way most of the organizers would like to keep it—never mind those few shady scandals among the Olympic committees of past and present, a bit of anabolic steroids here and there and a modicum of bad mouthing from one or two countries against the Aussie hosts. Unfortunately, we dare never forget that even with good things, the good is the enemy of the best, and the bottom line of the events still has to be, "I win; you lose." Hopefully good sportsmanship might prevail, but it's never ever guaranteed.

But before we depart this brief window on competitive sports, we ought to note that, when all is said and done, it does appear that humanism's ultimate playoff foe in the real Grand Finals, will most certainly be the Ancient of Days!

And the preferred games, I must yet add, is the Hebraic model expressed by Paul the Apostle, which needs no Bandaids™ for self-centered overtones:

> *But one thing I do: Forgetting what is behind and straining toward what is ahead, I press on toward the goal to win the*

prize for which God has called me heavenward in Christ Jesus (Philippians 3:13b-14).

In Paul's metaphoric challenge there are no losers—everyone has a "right" to win. This is hardly to knock the Olympics, which most of us truly do enjoy every four years, but to recognize and better measure where we are at personally in a society saturated with a built-in competitive spirit to survive the rat race. Perhaps with due introspection and repentance, we might even save ourselves from stomping out a few of our own self-designated "rats" in the process!

And then there are all the other patterns of a less than biblical competitive spirit woven throughout the fabric of our Western society that require little added elaboration. Most modern educational systems must foster achievement at the expense of that less fortunate fellow who has a hard time cutting it. In a few enlightened systems, however, student evaluation is being purposely withheld from public scrutiny for the very reason of protecting the underachiever from embarrassment. But even if it is successfully cloaked in the classroom, the day of educational reckoning comes sooner or later. There are winners, and there are losers.

So how can you protect the "loser" in a society of cutthroat competition, led primarily by the crafty and cunning winners in the Western world? Who is it that cannot well know that at the end of the day, his loss of future advancement was only at the gain of one stronger and more clever than himself? Indeed, is there any other underlying principle at work today in so-called ascension into the "real world"—in employment, in business and in the financial bloodletting in miniature to massive world markets across the planet? This is the labyrinth we have inherited in the Western world. This is a system from which we cannot readily escape.

The building blocks of humanism are competition—let there be no question. Cain and Abel who tested it, and the ancient Greeks who blessed it, are never far from our own arena. For over 2500 years, beginning with the man-centered insights of our Hellenistic "benefactors," humanity has practiced his slippery skills to quash his fellow kind. And when all is said and done, the obvious benefits and the presumed rightness of his cause makes man's competition with his Creator flow all the more smoothly, humanism being the new creed in the citadel, and Nietzsche's superman concept of the all powerful individual—the god-man if you will—the "glorious" end of it all. Unfortunately as we watch our god-man oriented world rapidly unraveling like a ball of yarn, that unhappy landing can logically only be a somewhat less-than-glorious anarchy!

But wait a minute. We forgot about that blissful abode in the Global Village! Surely these clever and cunning saviors of the globe must have these minor incidentals of human relationships all beautifully worked out. Before our hopes arise too high, perhaps I should reinforce a point made earlier. We will require some small explanation as to how it will be possible for one and all to have absolute freedom to crush his every other competitor en masse, yet all the while Liberation Village relaxes in peace and harmony? They must have worked out some guidelines in the fine print. Like what will happen if you are poor, or even a battler, or the wrong color, or a Jew, or a Bible-oriented Christian—or what if you're just a fetus? Oh no, not a just fetus!

Big Brother,[10] I fear, will need some beautifully big biceps to keep it all together, not to mention a constitution of stainless steel to never buckle under the "weaknesses" of compassion and sensitivity. So much for human freedoms.

The Pronoun Problem

Yet the alternative design of an extended and supportive family complete with an Abba who cares is a concept that today's futuristic society regards to be quite as dead as Abel. All the while NASA ironically searches the galaxies for preferred forms of distant life with little success to report thus far. One wonders if NASA might yet come up with a Hubble-class telescope that you could turn around and look into the wrong end like I used to do with those smaller jobs when I was a kid. And everything gets real little. We might be able to have a good look at ourselves with more realistic dimensions than the Greeks suggested. Who knows, we might learn something yet!

So while we wait for that, I think I'll go for an Almighty God and His original blueprint. Unfortunately, having been immersed—or is it baptized—in this self-centered, competition oriented, individualistic, uninhibited and God-insensitive society for so long, how do I find my way back?

Pronoun mix-ups! Competition with your fellows and competition with God—for a bigger slice of the pie with the former and overseeing the *whole* pie with the latter. It's ironic, but Someone once said something about those two circles of relationship, but it came out almost opposite:

> "Love the LORD your God with all your heart and with all your soul and with all your mind and with all your strength." The second is this: "Love your neighbor as yourself." There is no commandment greater than these (Mark 12:30-31).

And so much for a biblical precedent on competition!

1 Deuteronomy 14:23.
2 C.S. Lewis, *The Screwtape Letters* (New York, NY: Macmillan Publishing Company, Inc.,1973), p. 98.
3 Exodus 20:3.
4 Genesis 1:26-28.
5 1 John 2:15-16.
6 Genesis 4:1-16.
7 We refer again to an excellent overview of this entire development and how it affects today's thinking by Christian Overman, *Assumptions That Affect Our Lives* (Simi Valley, CA: Micah 6:8 Publishers, 1996); specifically "The Difference between Greek and Hebrew Thought," pp. 21-35; "Hebrew Family Values," pp. 120-128; "The Problem with Plato's Dualism" and "Tracing Plato through the Church," pp. 155-169. Overman's website is accessible on: www.biblicalworldview.com.
8 Even though the account of Cain and Abel is presented in the Hebrew Scriptures, it would be quite in error to associate this event with the Hebraic extended family code of conduct which God initiated through Abraham, and then specifically spelled out through Moses. Compare also David Bivin, *Understanding the Difficult Words of Jesus* (Shippensburg, PA: Destiny Image Publishers, 1982).
9 Overman, op. cit. "Who Makes the Snow, God or Mother Nature?"; "The Extraordinary Hebrew God," pp. 41-51.
10 Refer to the Big Brother concept in Orwell, op. cit.

CHAPTER 10
If God Loves Poor Folks, Why Not Make a Few More?

The Third World—or shall we call it the "developing world"—has been my backyard for some four decades. I know it well. For 40 years I have breathed in its cultural sensitivities.

Born in the Western world, I was educated initially in science and mathematics. Then after working for a number of years in nuclear energy, I made a most improbable professional flip. I bowed out of a reasonably lucrative career, which had had an even more attractive grand staircase to ascend the heights of fortune before me. Instead I returned to university and retooled to pursue linguistics, field anthropology and Bible translation, ultimately catapulting into the nearly unsullied— to foreign interests—rain forest of Papua New Guinea.

My new environs were not exactly affluent America, yet for the Third World it was well and truly five-star bush. Our very appropriate home had a lovely grass roof and an immaculate dirt floor, while the calling afforded such unique fringe benefits as mud, mosquitoes and malaria. But in striking contrast, the Abba I was learning to hear and follow proved to constitute an ever-comforting Presence never too far away.

The Waola tribe had seen their first steel only some four years before we arrived on the scene—their first nails, spades, hammers and bush knives. Their axes had been sharpened flint, their spades were but pointed sticks, their knives were a split and razor-sharp bamboo while their "nails" were vines collected from the rain forest, which bound the slim poles together for their simply constructed dwellings.

Ironically, the first wheels many of these highland dwellers ever encountered from the outside world were hardly on an ox cart, but on a 20th century single engine light aircraft, dropping in as it were from outer space onto often crudely and precariously constructed airstrips gouged out of treacherous mountain terrain. Simulating the touch of a TV remote control, we flipped from neutrons, protons and gamma rays into the unmistakable Stone Age. It proved a bit more than changing TV channels—this was real life!

In our first few years, we had for the first time ever deciphered the enigmatic Waola alphabet and searched out the grammar constructions of a reasonably complex language system. Their grammar, we discovered, afforded options of over 100 endings for any verb. Linguistics Lesson Number One: There is no such thing as a "primitive language."

We ultimately translated the Scriptures and published them along with corresponding quality texts to introduce the concept of literacy. We taught, established medical clinics, introduced mechanics, carpentry, and related Western innovations of obvious natural benefit. Yet we hoped to avoid those facets of a Western mindset, which our own society has thus far failed to come to terms with—like vindicated greed from the profusion of competitive spirits we considered in the previous chapter.

How well I recall those early milestones, struggling up mountain slopes splattered with mud, soaked with rain, out of breath, scanning the horizon, "Lord God Almighty, what in the world am I doing in this place?" But even before any divine whisper might choose to reecho, any alternative course to challenge this God-ordained opportunity was unthinkable. "No way, Lord, could I ever trade this hallowed classroom of human experience for all the glitter on the globe." You know what? We learned right along with our Stone Age family, and I guess that's what the rest of this chapter is all about.

At university, the one class I disdained most was economics. Economic theory—which I guess I always pigeon-holed as a sort of academic gambling—just didn't turn me on! Hey, I liked formulas like $E=mc^2$ or maybe $x + y =$ something-you-can-be-sure-of. But you know what else? Those Waola tribesman opened my eyes to the first good economics theory that really grabbed me:

No one is ever poor until his long-lost neighbor moves in with access to an inordinate amount of clam shells (read: big bucks) over what he has!

Now this is not to be confused with communism, whether spelled with either an upper case or lower case "c," because my Waola friends were hardly socialists. Nor am I sure why either Adam Smith or J. Maynard Keynes didn't come up with some suggestions on this one—the finesse to narrow the social gap rather than to widen it.(In actual fact, I really do know why.) But at this moment in history, I would that the rest of the West might at least somehow get a handle on it. In reality, it is more ethical than economic.

Another valuable lesson from their Stone Age "humanities department" was that human relationships held a long edge over the satisfaction of proving oneself right. What a unique opportunity it was to enter the heads and hearts of a society, which the sullied value system of the Western world had appraised as "primitive" simply on the scorecard of technical achievement! What an education to rub shoulders with a people that in most presumed measurements of progress, paralleled the era of Abraham, and at the same time, experience an invaluable value system long lost to the Atomic Age.

I didn't understand it all in the beginning, but over the years as we stood back and weighed our own cultural assumptions along with many of theirs, the pluses and minuses became abundantly clear. We found a people preserved from antiquity that had never been tainted with the Hellenistic mindset which had long before goaded ensuing generations in Europe and westward, to gear down to far greater matters than honoring God!

May I not be misunderstood. The hands of the Waolas were hardly clean from the array of sordid stains of any society anywhere, blemished with such iniquities as greed or jealousy, hatred, theft or violence. But what we did amazingly discover was the wealth of spiritual depth in their sensitivity to human relationships. In those days they possessed a unique value system, which sadly over the decades has been under constant threat by Western indulgences that never cease to worm their way in.

I shall never forget the indelible experience of reading the parable of the Prodigal Son[1] to my Waola neighbors for the very first time. I had just finished the translation into their vernacular and went outside to find someone with whom I could check out the response. Here was a group of ordinary, illiterate (at that early point of time) village bush guys just sitting and talking, so I sprang the new story on them. But you never finish these things without a comprehension test. So I said, "Okay, who was the bad guy in the story?" Without the slightest hesitation, an unmistakably chorused response was,

"The older brother!" A bit taken aback by the spontaneity I asked, "Why?" Again, the clear consensus, "Because he was jealous!" And that's what I mean about Stone Age sensitivities.

Moreover, the Waola vocabulary had words that not only expressed evil action toward one's fellow man, but scrupulously differentiated in terminology for the motivation for doing so! In fact, certain root meanings gave us a far greater range of nuances for implicit and dynamic Scripture translation than one could find in either the preceding Greek or English vocabulary.

Need I note that Abba ultimately made a reasonable impression in hundreds of village congregations throughout the Waola tribal homeland, not to mention tens of thousands more throughout the some 750 language demarcated not-so-united nations that make up the linguistic collage known as Papua New Guinea. Abba, it would appear, most fluently gets His point across in a Hebraic mindset.

Then one more astounding observation. Except for a divided Fiji,[2] there is not an iota of anti-Semitism throughout the non-Westernized and consequently non-Hellenized Pacific Islands. The first colonizers —commercial and otherwise—obviously forgot to tell them it's not "kosher" for the Gentiles to get too overly interested in Jews.

But times are changing—especially on the economic scene. The colonialism of the 18th and 19th centuries has taken on new shape in the last half of the 20th century. There's a new god on the global block, who writes love notes to his worshippers, mostly on 6" slips of numbered green and white paper—beginning with George Washington as No. 1 and proceeding on up to 1000!

To tell the truth, however, mammon is anything but new. It has held a fairly long tenure in one form or another ever since Fred Flintstone started trading clam shells with Johnny Hart's BC boys.

Papua New Guinea, along with all the rest of the other developing world, has gone quite commercial with an ever-widening gap between the Western educated elite and the masses of losers who never got off the starting blocks. May we note that in this noble assistance to the "backward" countries, there is just enough groomed aristocracy in the Third World to cement economic ties with the governments of the more developed nations, while the economic gap between rich and poor blows out to increasingly astronomical proportions. So much for the benevolent government "overseas aid packages" to the still struggling onlookers in the developing world.

But we must make a clear distinction between those occasional international aid organizations—most often Christian motivated—who, in clearly philanthropic pursuits, are over-extending themselves and their staff workers to genuinely and selflessly identify with the have-nots of the globe. Indeed, this is their life's purpose. These are still a contingent of caring folk around the world who do recognize the plight of the masses of the underprivileged and altruistically want to help. And they do. Sadly, we will find few if any politicians, governments or multinationals among them!

Why? In close scrutiny and by definition, we will find nearly 180-degree opposite agendas in their respective motivations. For a politician to stay a politician he needs money, and what's more, he needs to balance the budget of the funds that are already committed into his trust. He was elected to cut taxes, eliminate waste and prosper the economy, not to give away goodies to strangers. If he does, he gives away his job as well. When voters go behind that curtain, their fists are clenched on more things than that little marking pencil. Think about it. This is not the time for benevolence! So when you hear about "foreign aid," don't kid yourself. There is many an unspoken motive to keep the budget balanced in order for the "kingdoms of this world" to survive.

Let's have a glance for the moment at the financial upheavals of the nations within the last decade that have suffered devastating losses in their currency devaluation. There was Mexico and the Latin American giant, Brazil; there was Indonesia, Thailand, and Korea; there was Malaysia, and there was Papua New Guinea; even Japan, the bedrock economic anchor of Southeast Asia went through—and is still experiencing—stormy fiscal seas.

Yet they presumably all recovered. Did they really? How? Mind you, the average Westerner in the industrialized world notices little and cares less about those foreigners who speak differently, think differently and who for all we know, might as well reside in a different galaxy. Storm in a teacup! Where's my credit card—must run over to the mall before it closes!

Well, it's long past time we "average Westerners" woke up. We may not be all that relaxed once we realize which way our cruise ship is actually heading. I saw an op-ed article not long ago, by Martin Flanagan a columnist in the Melbourne Age, a more than prestigious Australian newspaper. The article on globalization was, indeed, of interest, but his title was even more intriguing: "Stop the McWorld, I want to get off."[3]

Let's just take a peek at those major Southeast Asian economies—as well as the plight of all the other developing nations whose economic stability over these last 10 years reeled and tottered with an eventual devastating devaluation of their respective currencies. After a time, the media moved on to other juicy debacles and we noted little more in the headline news. If they are "developing," what of their development now? Did they actually recover? Or did they all perish?

Over the last two or three centuries, almost all of these nations had been "developed" by colonial powers primarily from the Western European nations. They were taught to speak the European language of their colonizers, which in the jaundiced eyes of the conquerors was an unprecedented blessing. Now they could learn from the real world (read: Hellenistic mindset) with all the latent less than spiritual fringe benefits. As a linguist, Bible translator, and one dedicated to the cause of true indigenous advantage, I obviously view this as something much less than brilliant. Nevertheless, it is now history, and life moves on.

Certainly this would have given them the opportunity to be educated in the universities of their colonizers and learn the true motivation of life, namely getting ahead. Reflecting on our previous chapter, "Getting ahead of whom?" we might ask!

And above all—as the faithful of the imposing nations of bygone years would maintain—we can take them the Bible and make Christians out of the lot. It's not the worst idea, but at the same time I can see a myriad of flashing red lights. Any honest believer who takes the Scriptures seriously, must have learned well enough by now that the Holy Writ teaches neither sect nor system, neither builds a religious hierarchy nor affords an assembly line process for producing Christians. Some operations might possibly provide a few useful crutches en route, but the bottom line is always to develop a long-term relationship with Abba as well as with one's fellow man. The Divine Message is neither a catechism to be learned, nor—above all—the establishment of a system that will ultimately find itself in competition with the *real* Kingdom. Thus, if we take pause to reflect, too many well-meaning ventures at the time unfortunately overlooked that bottom line—a meaningful relationship with Abba!

Unfortunately, the Church in those days found themselves much too closely associated with the appetites of their own secular governments who professed a "development" that was geared to quite an unrelated agenda—developing the diamond mines, the gold mines, the timber, the teak, the rare minerals which Europe coveted, the copra, the sugar, the spices and the trade. You name it. It would appear that European bank accounts became even more highly developed than most of the less fortunate masses!

Of course, those "poor heathens" also got a slice of the pie—a very small slice, of course. And who ate it? Well, that's a problem. Obviously it was that tiny elite that mastered the language, education system, and worldview of their colonizers. And the greedy Hellenistic world bred two whole new echelons of haves and have-nots.

The major heartbreak to be observed is a present-day Africa, after some five decades of independence, whose cultural heart and soul has been ripped out. The masters of the colonial empires seemed to have had better success with their gospel of greed than the Bible schools who took opportunity to cling to the coattails of their respective secular governments. Today, with a new hierarchy of elite well in place, little has changed since the dubious colonial days except the color of the masters and the degree of oppression.

In the former days, the diseased, the despairing, and the destitute begged for crumbs on the footpaths. Today their blood runs in the street. Only the guard has changed.

Make no mistake, however. The faithful, the caring and those who march to the beat of a different drummer are still hard at work—perhaps harder than ever—reflecting their Abba with genuine care, good deeds and Good News. But their motivation represents quite another Kingdom than the previous colonial powers left in their wake.

If this reflection has seemed too "political" for some, perhaps it's apropos for a quote from the Prophet Nahum. It seems that some of the Almighty's spokesmen from over two millennia ago made similar "political" proclamations:

> *You have increased the number of your merchants till they are more than the stars of the sky, but like locusts they strip the land and then fly away. Your guards are like locusts, your officials like swarms of locusts that settle in the walls on a cold day—but when the sun appears they fly away, and no one knows where* (Nahum 3:16-17).

Not long ago the media reported the tragedy in war-torn Sierra Leone of the little lad whose foot was wantonly severed from his body by the machete of a crazed and mindless enemy. But this cannot be written off as a byproduct of a savage Africa gone wild. No way. It is from the marriage of the greed of a white colonialist West and the lust for power by a now fanatic segment of an uprooted and destabilized Black culture—the grotesque progeny of the worst of two worlds.

But after World War II, as this global conglomeration of colonies started acting up like a bunch of unruly teenagers, Europe began to reflect upon the folly of their ways (not sure if any genuine repentance really ever came to the fore!), and they were motivated to negotiate with the colonized. Perhaps it might be well if these independence-ignited multitudes sort of move out on their own now that they had come of age.

Moreover, the United States who freed her slaves decades before and whose morals were now far above such ignoble and repressive tactics (we won't mention the North American Indians who don't fit so neatly into the story!) strongly pressured those insensitive and maternally minded colonial powers in Europe to cease and desist from such archaic activities.[4] Thus it happened, and as a result we have today an explosion of independent nations such as the world had not seen since the building boom in Babel. Obviously, everyone is now happy. This has been the recipe to eliminate all wars and bloodshed, and certainly no more nefarious colonialism as we have seen in centuries gone by.

Never mind the wars and bloodshed. That's a bit embarrassing, so just look the other way. Instead, let's check up on progress in the really important areas—like economics.

Since 1990, the value of the Papua New Guinea monetary unit, the *kina*, fell to 30% of its former value. The Indonesian *rupia*, next door, plummeted even lower. And this was the repeated scenario of the last decade throughout all of Southeast Asia and other Latin American nations, particularly Mexico and Brazil.

The dust has long settled. Life goes on. Papua New Guinea is eating more of their staple—yams and sweet potatoes—than they ever have since their independence in 1975. Brazil and Mexico are back to more beans than ever before, while Southeast Asia is little different in diet, only nostalgia, and a McRice dream that never came any more flavorful than a bit more salt! The minority elite can still afford CDs, PCs and TVs because they have been catapulted to important connections, while the best connections the masses of their less fortunate countrymen can come up with are grass huts with mud floors, deteriorating Western constructed clinic buildings—with nary a bandaid or aspirin on their shelves—lovely new potholes in once paved roads and open sewage slithering down the streets. And the poor get much, much poorer.

Jesus said that we will always have the poor among us, and it would appear that there are not a few on the planet who do not have the slightest problem with that reflection![5] I think it was Abraham Lincoln who is credited with the observation that God must have certainly loved the poor people because he made so many of them. Indeed, you read the title to this chapter. Why not make a few more!

What happened to the Western aid of the last four decades following that illustrious dream of independence? First of all, anyone who lives in the grassroots of these places knows there is precious little "humanitarian aid" from the once colonialist governments, without very secure strings attached. In short, "We'll set you up in such a way that you will be in pole position to buy our products, employ our contractors and utilize—for cash, of course—all manner of our expert technical services." Shall we call it a financial yo-yo arrangement? Guess who holds the string? And when the currency crashes—go directly to square one, do not pass go, do not collect $200!

It's time for another Scripture verse. How about a relevant word from the Prophet Amos? True, he was declaring divine judgment upon his own people, but would the Almighty ever suggest immunity for any other oppressor in another day or at another time?:

> *Hear this, you who trample the needy and do away with the poor of the land,…buying the poor with silver and the needy for a pair of sandals, selling even the sweepings with the wheat…I will never forget anything they have done* (Amos 8:4, 6-7b).

And the Prophet Ezekiel decries the same crime as did a host of others throughout both the Old and New Testaments:

> *Now this was the sin…of Sodom: She and her daughters*

were arrogant, overfed and unconcerned; they did not help the poor and the needy (Ezekiel 16:49).[6]

But there's far more. These Third World governments had crushing financial burdens to resolve with the World Bank. They found themselves in such dire straits, they had no redress to even begin to touch the immense interest on their loans. Many also had monumental debts to multinational corporations who were "helping" develop their mines, their cities, their plush high-rise offices (that only foreign multinationals could afford to occupy) and exotic government buildings they could ill sustain, and which were light years away from the humanity they presumed to represent.

In a final grand gesture of redemption, the International Monetary Fund, along with the World Bank, comes one last time to the rescue with "humanitarian" cash in hand to deliver the destitute and the penniless from their perilous predicament. But to quote the Honorable Paul Hellyer, in his address to the Reclaiming Democracy Conference held in Sydney, Australia, in April 2000, a new reality surfaces:

"But then they attached conditions…, 'We will lend you money to keep you solvent, but *we want you to run your countries our way*, and we want you to cut back on your health care, and we want you to cut back on your educational expenditures, and we want you to balance your budgets, and we want you to lower your borders to imports, to reduce the tariffs and allow external imports, and *we want you to agree that foreigners can buy your assets*, and we want you to do all these things as conditions of the loans.' So in effect, they were saying, 'We're going to impose the Anglo-Saxon model, the economic model, on the rest of the world.'"[7]

Shall we call it neo-colonialism? This time around, however, the United States has now joined the "reformed" European colonial clique, and maintains, in fact, a very high profile in its direction.[8]

So much for freedom, fairness, equality, and justice in the developing nations. Red and yellow, black and white—their bosses now show up in expensive suits and ties in the international committee meetings, but no one is quite sure how their masses of destitute have-nots can ever be squashed to fit into the fantasized lifestyle of the Global Village. Perhaps they will have a tract of pristine jungle out back for hunting and gathering.

Actually that kind of lifestyle is not as bad as the blood baths until they look across at all those high rises in the Village, complete with swimming pools, malls, feature parks and all sorts of things that the haves take for granted but which "those kind of people" (the have-nots of course) wouldn't know how to use properly anyway, and therefore would never really miss.

One more quote on how the Ancient of Days sees it from His vantage point:

> *You hate the one who reproves in court and despise him who tells the truth. You trample on the poor and force him to give you grain. Therefore, though you have built stone mansions, you will not live in them; though you have planted lush vineyards, you will not drink their wine. For I know how many are your offenses and how great your sins. You oppress the righteous and take bribes and you deprive the poor of justice in the courts. Therefore the prudent man keeps quiet in such times, for the times are evil* (Amos 5:10-13).

Now that was a word from the Judge. Perhaps Rudyard Kipling might be chosen to best express a final statement representing the accused in the dock from his classic, *Gunga Din*:

"Though I've belted you and flayed you,
By the livin' Gawd that made you,
You're a better man than I am, Gunga Din!"[9]

1 Luke 15:11-32.

2 Fiji is the only indigenously governed South Pacific island nation with a large proportion of foreign immigrants, i.e. of non-Polynesian, non-Melanesian or non-Micronesian ethnicity. Great Britain, the colonial power in the 19th century brought masses of predominately Indian laborers into Fiji in 1879 creating a divided society, in contrast to her South Pacific neighbors who hold a generally uniform world view of biblical Christianity after initial roots in animism. *Encyclopaedia Britannica* (Macropaedia), Vol.7 (Helen Hemingway Benton, Publisher, Chicago, 1974), pp. 296.

3 "Stop the McWorld, I Want To Get Off," *The Age*, July 9, 1999.

4 Paul Hellyer, former Canadian Deputy Prime Minister, and current leader of the Canadian Action Party, in a lecture "Global Finance: Dismantle or Reform?" delivered at the Reclaiming Democracy Conference, Sydney, Australia, April 2000. Full text of the address was rebroadcast on Australian ABC's Background Briefing, May 30, 1999 and may be accessed in its entirety on: www.abc.net.au/rn/talks/bbing/index.

5 Matthew 26:11.

6 For biblical injunction against oppression of the defenseless see also Jeremiah 22:13: Amos 5:21-24; Malachi 3:5; and James 5:2-5.

7 Hellyer, op. cit. Refer also to Paul Hellyer, *Stop:Think* (Toronto: Chimo Media, 1999); See also Catherine Caulfield, *Masters of Illusion: The World Bank and the Poverty of Nations* (NY: Henry Holt Company, 1996) and Michel Chossudovsky, *The Globalisation of Poverty: Impacts of IMF and World Bank Reforms* (Penang: Third World Network, 1997).

8 Ibid.

9 Rudyard Kipling, *Gunga Din and Other Favourite Poems* (United Kingdom: Dover Thrift Editions, 1991).

CHAPTER 11

An Ark...or Anarchy?

At the time of this writing, the diminutive state of Israel, after two millennia of exile, is struggling to preserve her precarious 53-year tenure of resurrection. Her Islamic adversaries outnumber her 100 to 1, and swear by Allah they will eventually achieve her ultimate destruction. Terrorist groups such as Hamas, Hizbullah, Islamic Jihad, and Fatah's Tanzim militia are currently armed to the teeth and flourishing within her borders under the protection of a now self-governing Palestinian Authority. The Palestinians are quite winning the media war of propaganda and disinformation, while terrorist Arafat under a Nobel Peace Prize facade is engineering the entire evil scheme, chuckling all the way to the armory.

At this point of his duplicity in a feigned "peace process," a logical thing for Israel to do is to work toward the abrupt removal of a conniving Mr. Arafat from the control panel of the so-called "peace talks." But would it be all that logical? He has so crafted his pinnacle perch that should he ever be eliminated, only terrorist vigilante groups would remain.

The only thing worse than a terrorist tyrant is no leadership whatsoever, where the regime of violence explodes into a multitude of mini-despots each with a bomb, a gun, a knife, or in the volatile Middle East scenario, far more deadly weapons than these petty tools of destruction. Systems such as these have the potential to degenerate from one consolidated arch-enemy to the dread setting where no one in your neighbor-hood—not to mention your own household—dare be trusted. That, indeed, is hell on earth.

God's prophets spoke of days like these, while Jesus saw fit to reemphasize the warning numerous times in His teaching:

> *For a son dishonors his father, a daughter rises up against her mother, a daughter-in-law against her mother-in-law— a man's enemies are the members of his own household* (Micah 7:6).[1]

This, of course, is the backdrop into which the Ancient of Days saw fit to replant an Israel re-gathered into a sea of her most vitriolic adversaries. By the time of publication and dis-tribution of this book, the crisis in Israel may well have deteri-orated even further. Arabic and Jewish homes and communities are interspersed in a kaleidoscope of interaction. It is hardly a land problem, but is a family hate problem be-tween ancient brothers, Ishmael and Isaac, which has been fostered and festering for nearly 4000 years. Civil war is a dev-astation, but unbridled anarchy is something even far worse.

Though this may be the oldest, the most irresolvable and the highest profile outline for uncontrollable violence in the days before us, it is hardly in isolation across the planet. Take the Balkan states with the volatile mix of Western worldview versus Slavic culture, and mix it with a broiling cauldron of Croatian, Serbian, and Islamic causes and you are at another flash point. In the last decade, world attention has been drawn to territorial disputes in Bosnia, Kosovo and most recently in Macedonia, but the world has been less informed on the root causes of Islamic insistence on independent status in this inseparable concoction of rival ethnicities struggling together. For those not much into history, this was hardly a new phenomenon that began in the days after World War II. The area has been a smoldering volcano following the European-Islamic Crusades of nearly one thousand years continuity. The fuse for World War I, in fact, was lit in Sarajevo with the assassination of the Archduke of Austria.[2] But, of course, a neat Global Village scenario would wipe out these prickly problems of fratricide forever, would it not? Or within the interpersonal proximity of a shrinking globe, would it only make it worse? Much worse! Battlefields have boundaries. Anarchy recognizes not even the sanctity of a front door.

In yet another continent, the tribal bloodletting in post-colonial Africa—which we have already pondered in previous contexts—is one more frightening spectacle of fragmenting communities. The media grapples for sensational stories for a time, but eventually the sensation fades, the ratings drop and the world once more looks the other way as Africa bleeds on. It would be nice if it would go away, but it doesn't. The disturbing point is that it is even edging ever closer to home— wherever that may be across the planet.

The crisis with fewest boundaries of all, however, is the collapse of democracy as we have initially observed in Chapter 2. Years ago, the Soviet Union perpetuated the observation that within democracy are the seeds of its own destruction. True, Soviet Communism caved in first, but this was hardly to negate their prediction for Western perpetuated constitutional democracy which, when the moment of truth is ultimately faced, was more than true.

A valid democratic system can work only if the principal players jointly agree to the rules of the game. If there is no basic understanding to the bottom line of give and take—as would be the case in attempting to negotiate with the theo-cratic or even secular Islamic dictatorships around the globe—forget it! I say this not even as a judgment of Islam, but as an analysis. If Islam is to be its own identity, it dare not compro-mise with any other "inferior" infidel system. As we noted in Chapter 1, the root linguistic meaning of "Islam" is "submis-sion." And again the question, who all do you suppose they have in mind that ultimately must submit to Allah?

Therefore, pretending a "democratic election" for these Islamic-oriented systems—one sixth of the world's popula-tion—is pure stage play for the benefit of whatever govern-ment has a need for pulling a wool balaclava over their own eyes or the eyes of their people. Thus, we come to a rock and a hard place, or as King Abdulla of Jordan in one recent circum-stance so succinctly expressed it, "Iraq and a hard place!"

In short, constitutional democracy becomes a travesty once the "constitution" shifts off the moral or ethical base of its founding, and thus—enter stage right—the seeds of its own demise. It can vote for itself a most lovely tombstone if it likes. Or if the political correctness of the hour has shifted to a grand coalition of personal indulgences, the "human rights" of splinter interests can conceivably hold sway over a dumb-founded 49% who, in the process, will be duly spat upon. Does any of this sound familiar? In fact, once the rules of the game are re-written—or should we say re-legislated—the tombstone becomes inevitable whether voted in or not.

If the Hellenistic concept of democracy introduces the premise that everyone—good or evil—has his legitimate voice in the universe, the logical conclusion of the matter—and the Greeks were no strangers to logic—must be that given enough time with an expanding cacophony of innumerable voices, the last word will ultimately be anarchy.

In retrospect, if everyone has his individual say, some-where along a more recent line of history this mutated to the presumption that everyone also has his legitimate rights. That doesn't sound too bad—quite democratic, in fact! But if everyone has rights, what happens when my rights conflict with your rights? Of course, we vote. That's the fair way to go.

Not always. I also have my right to protest. That means if I don't like the decision, I have to get a bit more forceful to demonstrate for my rights to prove that my rights are more po-litically correct than your rights. This includes "peaceful demonstrations," which in the Middle East—by openly de-clared and straight-faced PLO definition—includes throwing rocks and firebombs, much of which is done by children so en-listed for the cause![3] It also includes the "right" to instill within the minds of 12-year-old kids the responsibility to be-come suicide bombers if it is for the destruction of Jews.[4]

But that's okay, they have their rights to be racist. Anyway, on the other side are always the racists, by definition of what we mean by "my rights." Democratic "rights" at this point have taken on a healthy measure of force—and may we never forget the finance. This is particularly so with the "con-stitutional democracy" that is now being exported to every culture across the globe by the currently controlling forces who would have us believe that it is quite a good thing. Unfortunately, the current "democratic system" as champi-oned by the Western powers, neither fits nor benefits the very diversely structured cultures in much of the Third World—an-other recipe for ultimate chaos.

Of course, I realize that the Middle East is an extreme ex-ample and quite far away from, let us say, Oklahoma City or the World Trade Center in New York, for instance! Anyone who knows their history has long ago observed that yesterday's exceptions are tomorrow's rules. Lest anyone not notice, the basis of global democracy as currently packaged and exported by the Western world (as if it were from God Himself), no longer has a foundation of understood values, morals and ethics, give and take.

Indeed, within democracy are the seeds of its own destruction. And the ultimate demise of a truly "democratic" globe is everyone having his own say. And, of course, that is a non-starter for peaceful coexistence. Then when lawless disintegration enters full bloom, it will be hell before the time—just like the book of Revelation foretells.

We already have previews with insubordinate gangs in many of the huge inner city metropolises around the globe. We have other matinee runs of uncontrollable violence world-wide, a recent example of which was played out in my own general environment of Southeast Asia. Irresponsible and unchecked militia gangs ran rampant with axes, clubs and machetes throughout East Timor.[5] The dust has settled only slightly, and the bloodletting is still an ever-present specter in the shadows. At the moment the media focus has gone to greener (or is it redder) pastures, but the fear and uncertainty certainly has not. Bloody uprisings throughout Indonesia continue to sweep this politically unstable island archipelago, the fourth most populous nation in the world.

The seeds of mob rule are germinating throughout the once colonialized world—the "developing" world—and are ominously edging ever westward.

Dare we mentally reflect on the anti-government, anti-globalization, anti-world finance, anti-ethnic riots that have been coursing our planet in uncomfortably recent days? One of the earliest ones in the current series was Seattle in the USA, soon echoed by Melbourne in Australia. And then there was the massive protest in Prague, and on to an even greater violent uprising in Stockholm. Our media cameras then swung to the ugly scenario of nasty racial explosions in the UK, next to the gory scenes of political protest in a westernized and democratic Jamaica. And the most recent catastrophic and destructive violence of all has been in Genoa, Italy, where the eight most powerful and supposedly influential men on the globe were only trying to have a little chat together.

If they are, indeed, in charge of this place, I'm not sure why they allow the revelers to make such a mess outside—every time. Each time these little parties go on—and it looks like they are getting more frequent—someone always seems to get it cleaned up afterward. I'm not sure who pays for it, however, but it won't be the mob that messed it up!

So where to next? And to what degree? And for what duration? And to what irreversibility with regard to the lengthening shadows of our day? Is this the "democratic freedom" we have all been pinning our hopes on?

Of course, these are only the "peaceful protests," mind you, expressed by mild mannered citizens (some are even professionally trained protesters) with only an ax to grind. We have not even considered the Osama bin Ladens of a mushrooming fundamentalist camp who have instead a score to settle, and who are patiently waiting in the wings for their day of opportunity to arrive.

This is anarchy—the fruits of civil liberties, of human rights, the flowering of unlimited freedom of speech, and the freedom to curse the God who created us—all coming to harvest time. This is Hellenism; this is humanism so ripe it is rotten. The eight most mighty leaders in the world could only click their tongues and shake their heads in disbelief!

But this is getting frighteningly depressing. What say we

talk about something else? So where do we go from here? What about the radical suggestion of trying God?

The Bible—the Hebrew Scriptures—is not an archaic record of nationalistic stories of a renegade desert tribe who outmaneuvered old Pharaoh, went on a prolonged safari and finally made it big by whipping a collection of Canaanite cults out of their senses. Nor does the Old Testament—the Jewish *Tanach*—climax with a whimpering record of I-hope-so Hebrew prophets, who smarting under the chastisement of their deity, continue to hang on to "one more go" for big glory once the desert dust settles.

Let's pause for a moment of truth. The Bible is not exclusively a book about Jews. Nor is even it a book about how you and I (and the Jews) can discover the right fire escape for another world. It's a book about God.

It reflects the principles of an infinite and inexpressible Creator—principles or covenants, if you wish—that work either for or against the family He chose to represent Him and reflect Him, as well as for or against all the rest of us who would presume to identify with Him. Moreover, those same principles will ultimately crush any and all who shake their fists at His resolve and His authority.

Everyone who falls on that stone will be broken to pieces,
but he on whom it falls will be crushed (Luke 20:18).

The Scriptures are a record of the one and only deity of the universe who is bound to have the last word with His creation. It is not simply humanity's handbook. It's about Him.

Even in secular circles, the story of Job has been a classic literary rendition from time immemorial. But in this generation of apostasy it may not be so well known, as Satan makes his final thrust into a humanistic society "come of age," ripping to shreds anything that would conflict with his final hellish assault on the authority of the King of the Universe.[6] Job's account is unrivaled in expression as the Almighty rests His case with this unfortunate human sufferer:

> *Then the* LORD *answered Job out of the storm. He said: "Who is this that darkens my counsel with words without knowledge? Brace yourself like a man; I will question you, and you shall answer me. Where were you when I laid the earth's foundation? Tell me, if you understand. Who marked off its dimensions? Surely you know! Who stretched a measuring line across it? On what were its footings set, or who laid its cornerstone—while the morning stars sang together and all the angels shouted for joy?"* (Job 38:1-7).[7]

And for the predominate theme of His unassailable sovereignty, He thunders over 60 times through His Prophet Ezekiel: "AND THEN WILL THEY KNOW THAT I AM THE LORD."[8]

May we continue our pause in our confrontation with truth. If we can adjust our egos ever so slightly, the Scriptures—both Old and New Testaments—were not preserved to primarily focus on our redemption. That could involve a tinge of humanistic assumption inherited distinctly from our ancient Greek detractors. The divine record focuses first and foremost directly on our Redeemer and it is only His mercy that brings the rest of us mortals into the larger picture of a caring Abba's designed redemption for His creation.

So, with regard to the prospects of our worldwide social order violently disintegrating as we watch from the front door, what we are already seeing and hearing around us, mixed with the accuracy of the ancient prophets does get a bit uncomfortable. Right? Well, our great Abba, in His loving kindness for all of His projected family, long ago surveyed a similar scene in the days of Noah and put His order in for an ark:

> *But Noah found favor in the eyes of the LORD. Noah was a righteous man, blameless among the people of his time, and he walked with God…Now the earth was corrupt in God's sight and was full of violence. God saw how corrupt the earth had become, for all the people on earth had corrupted their ways. So God said to Noah, "I am going to put an end to all people, for the earth is filled with violence because of them. I am surely going to destroy both them and the earth. So make yourself an ark of cypress wood"* (Genesis 6:8, 9b, 11-14a).

That was a few years back. Probably a bit too long for the New World Order folks to remember. But Jesus jogged the memories of the do-it-yourself leadership of His day—along with all the faithful—when He suggested it wasn't all over yet:

> *Just as it was in the days of Noah, so also will it be in the days of the Son of Man. People were eating, drinking, marrying and being given in marriage up to the day Noah entered the ark. Then the flood came and destroyed them all. It was the same in the days of Lot. People were eating and drinking, buying and selling, planting and building. But the day Lot left Sodom, fire and sulfur rained down from heaven and destroyed them all. It will be just like this on the day the Son of Man is revealed* (Luke 17:26-30).

Anyway, the world has since returned to square one when it comes to wanting to get rid of their Maker, but don't forget the ark, my friends.

However, there is not only one ark in the Divine Message, but two. The second one is described in the second book of Moses:

> *And they shall make an ark of acacia wood; two and a half cubits shall be its length, a cubit and a half its width, and a cubit and a half its height. And you shall overlay it with pure gold, inside and out you shall overlay it, and shall make on it a molding of gold all around…You shall make a mercy seat of pure gold; two and a half cubits shall be its length and a cubit and a half its width. And you shall make two cherubim of gold; of hammered work you shall make them at the two ends of the mercy seat…And the cherubim shall stretch out their wings above, covering the mercy seat with their wings, and they shall face one another; the faces of the cherubim shall be toward the mercy seat. You shall put the mercy seat on top of the ark, and in the ark you shall put the Testimony that I will give you. And there I will meet with you, and I will speak with you from above the mercy seat, from between the two cherubim which are on the ark of the Testimony, about everything which I will give you in commandment to the children of Israel (Exodus 25:10-11, 17-18, 20-22).[9]*

Hebrew uses two different words for "ark." *Tebah* refers to Noah's cruise liner; *aron* is the term used for the golden Ark of the Covenant as detailed in the text above. Both are translated as "ark" in almost all English translations, which is quite legitimate. The root meaning in each case is a protective covering, chest or shielding enclosure. One can easily appreciate the relationship between the two terms.

A most interesting parallel usage of Noah's concealment from devastation is the little woven rescue basket fashioned

for the infant Moses to spare him from the genocidal proclamation of Pharaoh.[10] This is the only other instance in
Scripture where *tebah* is used as a covering for deliverance
from disaster.

So what of the impending turmoil that is threatening our
globe like a massive tidal wave—the lawlessness, the pornography that hackers slip into unsuspecting web sites to rape our
minds with unforgettable filth? What of the graffiti that of-
fends the decency of one and all until you try to suppress it,
presuming it no longer affects you? What of the video games of
violence beyond sane comprehension, movie themes of canni-
balistic sadism that would make Sodom and Gomorrah vomit,
and massively best-selling children's books that are nothing
but demonic saturation of young impressionable minds? A re-
vealing article in Singapore's *Sunday Times* presented the
above filth as deep concerns of the Communist Party of a secular China that is working overtime to keep these macabre
Western innovations out of the hands of their kids.[11] Even the
morals of atheists are quite above the satanic saturation of our
"free world" society today. Doesn't anyone ever bother to
pause and reflect on why China—which is cynically down-
graded as being "poor on human rights"—is so bent on
keeping those "glorious freedoms" of the Western World well
away from their shores?

All of these are but a fractional expression of the mental
and spiritual anguish that is engulfing the planet. Creeping
ever closer to home is the physical threat of violence and ter-
rorism that no longer recognizes international boundaries.[12] In
fact, those boundaries of the Western world have become an
impassioned challenge to the venomous hatred of an offended
Islam with a thinly veiled agenda for ultimate world domina-
tion. After nearly six decades of reflection, the original nu-

clear powers of the West have grown to loathe the thought of a nuclear decimation of millions of humankind. The new players, itching to get off the bench and into the ball game, unfortunately have not.

It's a bit grim out there, folks! That's probably why most sane citizens say (read: hope), "It certainly can't happen here!"

So in all of this we have two arks in front of us. Which one will you go for? (Not that you get a choice.) The big one, of course! The Noah job! Well, have you started building it? The old one is a bit kaput. Someone found a couple lines in the geography alongside a mountain in Turkey a while back, and they reckon that's it. They may be right, but it's going to take a fair bit of fixing before you could get it going again. In fact, aren't you glad the Most High didn't tell you to build a boat? I'm sure most in your fellowship group would have even given you a hand, but even then the prospects of getting it up and floating aren't all that great. That first ark was Act I, remember, but now we are in Act III, and the drama is almost over.

You know, a lot of people thought they were going to be out of here in a type of the ark and soaking up the heavenly sunshine long before this nasty stuff we've been talking about ever got off the ground. But checking the flood of filth and evil all around us, we are up to our knees already and it's getting deeper by the day. Better we do our homework on that first type of redemptive ark.

Noah was never more than a foot from the deluge at any one time and in no way drifted off into the celestial. He hit pay dirt on Ararat and probably didn't even walk home. He *was* home! Another clue: Noah never even got his feet wet. A few lines above I mentioned knees, and I check again and the flood is rising so fast I can't even see my knees anymore!

It's time for Plan B.

What about this smaller golden ark with the two golden cherubim on top with wings touching each other? I mean, it's impressive, but what on earth can I do with that?

Let's check it out:

Behind the second curtain was a room called the Most Holy Place, which had the golden altar of incense and the gold-covered ark of the covenant. This ark contained the gold jar of manna, Aaron's staff that had budded, and the stone tablets of the covenant. Above the ark were the cherubim of the Glory, overshadowing the atonement cover (Hebrews 9:3-5).

That first ark was a massive umbrella. This second one is even more powerful. The Greek mindset asks, "How do I describe God? How can I explain Him? How can I decipher His plans?" The Hebraic mind much more simply says, "What does He do?" Look in the golden box. That's what He does. The manna is His provision. The rod that budded is His miraculous deliverance. The stone tablets, His covenant relationship with a people He loves and can never forget:

But Zion said, "The LORD has forsaken me, the Lord has forgotten me." "Can a mother forget the baby at her breast and have no compassion on the child she has borne? Though she may forget, I will not forget you! See, I have engraved you on the palms of my hands; your walls are ever before me" (Isaiah 49:14-16).

That was the meaning. He wanted to lodge with them. This is the meaning. He wants to abide with us. And in the same breath, the ancient Israelites didn't just do laps around

Mount Sinai with a bit of impressive—and very heavy—ancient artwork. *They walked the distance with their God!*

That impressive golden ark was hardly an idol to be polished, an icon to be admired, or even a Bible to be bashed. Instead, this is a reminder to My people of who I AM.

There is no theory, no creed, no formula, no immortalized lifestyle, no self-crucifixion or personal pinnacle of perfection to conquer at this moment of time. Only an Abba relationship with the Most High will keep your feet dry in the rising tide.

Now living under the shadow of the Almighty is not that hard to come by. The problem is that too many of us have been taught to pant and slog up the wrong side of the mountain under our own steam, or—in the extreme alternative—to put our brains to bed and toboggan down the wrong shimmering slopes. Except for the massive mercy of God, neither works all that well.

In what I perceive as a major late-in-the-day call to a slumbering and callused church, the world witnessed a mighty Holy Spirit awakening and renewal in the 1960s and 1970s. Unfortunately, large numbers of both the Hill Climbers Chapel and the Toboggan Fellowship Group missed the boat. (Note I did not dare say ark!) The movement was neither a measurement on how many gifts you did or did not have, nor on how many tongues you could manage nor on how high you could jump. Certainly *all* manner of gifts were involved in a myriad of settings, but it was never the primary purpose of the Almighty to highlight spiritual toys to be flaunted by any or all of the otherwise spiritually insecure. The focus was on the King of the Universe Himself and not on any or all tools He gives to His laborers to get the final job done. The Holy Spirit movement of those days was geared directly to arouse sleeping saints and to establish a twilight call to intimate relationship with the

Most High. To multitudes it gave an added dimension to the indelible pronouncement of John the Baptist:

> *I baptize you with water, but he will baptize you with the Holy Spirit* (Mark 1:8).

From all walks of the spiritual spectrum, many identified with the call and drew closer to Abba—much closer.

Unfortunately, there were always a few who shot off on tangents with newfound phenomena while yet others blazed off after them with bundles of Bible texts in hand, prepared to yet administer one more baptism to the obviously errant—the baptism of fire!

It would hardly have been necessary. Nevertheless, both of the marginal dissident factions seemed to have sadly missed the point of God-ordained intimacy with Abba. Other than a bit of "Daniel faith," it's not all that hard.

> *Then King Nebuchadnezzar leaped to his feet in amazement and asked his advisers, "Weren't there three men that we tied up and threw into the fire?" They replied, "Certainly, O King." He said, "Look! I see four men walking around in the fire, unbound and unharmed, and the fourth looks like a son of the gods.… So Shadrach, Meshach and Abednego came out of the fire, and…(they) crowded around them. They saw that the fire had not harmed their bodies, nor was a hair of their heads singed; their robes were not scorched, and there was no smell of fire on them* (Daniel 3:24-25,26b-27).

If my priorities are in place, it's God's problem, not mine.

Soon His Messiah will again appear, and even before His feet once again touch the Mount of Olives[13] we will have joined him to consider the daily manna, the incredible delivery miracles, and the eternal covenant, which time and again He ends up mercifully offering to keep both sides of the bargain:

> *I will sprinkle clean water on you, and you will be clean; I will cleanse you from all your impurities and from all your idols. I will give you a new heart and put a new spirit in you; I will remove from you your heart of stone and give you a heart of flesh. And I will put my Spirit in you and move you to follow my decrees and be careful to keep my laws. You will live in the land I gave your forefathers; you will be my people, and I will be your God* (Ezekiel 36:25-28).

1 See also Matthew 10:21, 34-36; Mark 13:12; Luke 12:51-53.

2 *The New Encyclopaedia Britannica* Vol.19 (USA: Encyclopaedia Britannica, Inc. 1974), p. 942.

3 "Palestinians Enlist Children for Jihad," *ICEJ Middle East Digest News Service*, March 19, 2001. See also a major collection of actual training photographs on www.projectonesoul.com.

4 Ithmar Marcus (Palestinian Media Watch): "Sweet Fragrance of Martyrdom," Arutz-7, May 17, 2001.

5 "Mayhem in East Timor Draws Threats of Intervention," *International Herald Tribune*, September 8, 1999.

6 See Revelation 12:12.

7 For appreciation of the entire dialogue see Job 38:1-42:6.

8 Some 60 references in Ezekiel are divided between: "Then they will know that I am the Lord" (Eze. 36:38) or "Then you will know that I am the Lord" (Ezekiel 37:6), along with over 20 additional references throughout the Scriptures varying slightly as "Then will all people know" "Then will the heathen know" or "Then will Israel know that I am the Lord."

9 Quoted from NKJV.

10 Ex. 2:1-4.

11 "China Set to Outlaw Popular Grotesque Toys: Fake mucus, blood and even X-rated toys seem to be favorite teen playthings, forcing parents and the authorities to look at banning them," *Singapore: The Sunday Times*, Feb. 18, 2001.

12 See paragraph on the disappearance of international boundaries in Chapter 3 pp. 27-28 as reported from: "Are We Coming Apart or Together?" by Pico Iyer, *Time*, May 22, 2000.

13 Zechariah 14:1-5

EPILOGUE

So what have we said? Or just closing our eyes and meditating for a moment, what all have we seen?

From the mighty global governments of the day to a fantasy One World village, from stage managed worldwide politics to a mind-bending media, from a planet physically under demolition to a globe that is becoming morally and spiritually perverted by the moment—where do we go from here?

Are there really any good answers? Or more precisely, are we really actually awaiting an answer? Is the too-hard basket all too convenient, while the confidence type of basket that once sheltered young Moses, far too risky to contemplate? Do we prefer to import buckets of sand from the beach for the OEDC—that is, the Ostrich Escape & Denial Club?

As the once familiar world crumbles around us at an accelerating pace, what insights can we glean from the Old Testament prophets? Or have they long passed their use-by dates? But should that be the case, what can we say of the one known as the Son of Man? Was He also dating Himself when He constantly quoted these "hardliners" of modern media mentality? After all, their messages were recorded in the only Scriptures the Teacher from Galilee ever had access to. Wouldn't that have limited the King of the Jews a bit in the research materials available at the time? Obviously these days the Internet offers us a fair bit more in the way of universal savvy!

In much more serious and sobering reflection, multitudes within our society have long come to this conclusion. Many may not admit it, but priorities, worldview and lifestyle unmistakably shout it from the housetops.

We certainly ought to be aware by now that there are a few more than just one unmarked garden path lying in wait for the less than watchful wanderer. Over the last two centuries, the church has found herself in a deluge of self-styled end of days prophetic updates, which presumably was to have taken a few of the rough edges off of what Jesus once seemed to have said.

Unfortunately, these excursions away from what the King and the prophets had warned us about, do not now appear to be nicely following the script of how we had supposed everything would neatly fall into place in the final act of the age! Thus, when all is said and done, it might not be a bad idea to go back to those ancient prophets who, quite frankly, provided a significant input into the very words of Jesus Himself. So in actual fact, the closer we get to a soon-to-come Middle East explosion—which few can deny will merit the credentials for WW III—the clearer it becomes that it is not only the world media that has surreptitiously kept us from the whole truth. How could we have been so misled twice in one day?

So instead of a self-serving and self-advised "spiritual" agenda—be it plodding up mountains of our own imaginations, or, even more energetically, building carnal "religious" castles out of self-effort—these are the days for which Bible believers should have been holding our collective breath. Distraction to our own "spiritual fulfillment" certainly must be a disappointment to Someone up there!

Why is it so hard to recognize that behind a smoke screen of international politics the core issue of the Middle East is four millennia of hatred à la Uncle Ishmael, and reinforced with 1300 added years of Islam. The trauma those recently resurrected dry bones of Israel has inflicted upon her legion of Arab adversaries is neither ethnic per se, nor is it a problem of land, or settlers or any other political presumption whatsoever.

Rather the roots of the frenzied conflict, which spans not a few millennia of unabated bloodletting long before the 20th century, is an ongoing metaphysical clash to someday settle whose version of God is superior—a concept quite clearly spelled out in the Bible from the Baals onward. And it is one that was hardly hidden to the worldview of the ancients. It is the God of creation—the God of the Bible—versus any and all rivals!

Interestingly enough, in these days of high-tech spirituality, we have one more new candidate for competition that has surfaced to create an interesting new global game of triangular chess. Since it is deemed less than brilliant for genuine gods to do battle—or "quarreling religions" as many folks seem to express their armchair understanding of the problem—the wisdom of the day is to overrule the claims of both the Eternal One and any other challengers. Hellenism come of age would prefer to demonstrate whatever moral superiority there may be in a much more logical and much less restricting system of secular humanism. Why not be God ourselves, and play Moses-the-lawgiver as we go along?

The only problem is that one of those two original contestants happens to be my Abba—and yours, if I read you correctly. And it's not my chessboard, it's His. And I'm not playing—the Most High is! And those of us who call Him "Abba" are just standing behind Him watching and waiting to see Him put all those other phony kings in check. Whoever heard of a chess player disclosing his moves almost 3000 years in advance? You have to be pretty good to do that!

So as we began this little wrap-up, what next? Where do we go from here? For the truly wise, it's never too late to make a few final in-course corrections. The prophets who impressed Jesus might even still have a few clues for us!

And as the curtain descends on the final showdown of the Almighty with His two last day challengers, it might be well to do a bit of inventory on whether—at the least—we may have been a bit naively sympathetic to either one of His adversaries, or—at the worst—have we even unwittingly been participating ourselves in carnal, self-serving humanism. In either case, at the end of the day, less than total allegiance to the real King of kings can only serve to aid and abet the antagonist. And with all of that—God forbid—we lose our focus and miss the boat!

Sorry, I'm going to have to run now—Abba promised me a bit more prime time with Him whenever I got this book finished!

For international ministry schedules, requests for meetings, or additional books, contact:

South Pacific Island Ministries, Inc.
P.O. Box 990, Smithfield 4878, Qld. Australia
Fax: (07) 4058-0258   International: (617) 4058-0258
E-mail: SpimAust@aol.com

BOOK SALES IN USA:
Available from your favorite Christian bookstore,
distributor, or online bookseller

Bulk sales to churches or non-profit organizations (10+ copies):
SPIM, Inc. Attention: Bernhard Laubli
Fax: (520) 962-8780 E-mail: spimusa@mindspring.com

BOOK SALES IN AUSTRALIA:
Wholesale orders from: W.A. Buchanan & Co., P.O. Box 206,
Geebung 4034 Qld., Tel: (07) 3865 2222 Fax: (07) 3865 2600
E-mail: service@wab.com.au
or available through Christian bookshops in your local area

BOOK SALES IN ISRAEL:
The Galilee Experience, P.O. Box 1693, Tiberias 14115
Tel. 04-672-3260 Fax: 04-672-3195
E-mail: info@TheGalileeExperience.com
or
Immanuel Bookshop (Associated with Christ Church)
P.O. Box 14037, Jaffa Gate, Jerusalem 911140
Tel: 02-626-4090 Fax: 02-626-3855
E-mail: christch@netvision.net.il
or
International Christian Embassy Jerusalem
Resources Center, 20 Rachel Imeinu St.
PO Box 1192, Jerusalem 91010
Tel: 02-539-9700 Fax: 02-566-9970
E-mail: icej@icej.org

ABOUT THE AUTHOR

VICTOR SCHLATTER was educated as a nuclear chemist at Purdue University. After 7 years in the halls of science, he pursued a new calling. He and his wife Elsie spent the next 30 years in Papua New Guinea where they translated the New Testament and parts of the Old Testament. Their work was prepared for publication with the Wycliffe Bible Translators and published in 1978 by the Bible Society of Papua New Guinea.

During these years, they planted the Tiliba Christian Church, which spread throughout tribal areas. It currently numbers almost 100 congregations with some 10,000 believers. They have also been involved in medical ministry, community development, and a literacy outreach.

Victor is the director of South Pacific Island Ministries and is the South Pacific islands representative to the International Christian Embassy in Jerusalem. He has made repeated trips to Jerusalem and continues his research on the biblical significance of the days in which we live, particularly as it relates to Israel. He travels extensively and lectures worldwide with a special sensitivity to the needs of the Third World.

His first book, *Where Is the Body?*, was published by Destiny Image in 1999 and is now in its third printing. This current work, *Showdown of the Gods,* focuses on the world's challenge to the God of the Bible by both secular humanism and Islamic terror. Ironically, *Showdown of the Gods* went to press on September 11, 2001.